The Spiritual Awakening Process

Coming Out of the Darkness and Into the Light

Christine Hoeflich

The Spiritual Awakening Process: Coming Out of the Darkness and Into the Light

© 2017 by Christine Hoeflich

All Rights Reserved. No part of this publication may be reproduced in any form or by any means, including scanning, photocopying, or otherwise without prior written permission of the copyright holder, except as provided under Fair Use provisions outlined by the U.S. Copyright Law.

Between Worlds Publishing
P.O. Box 67458
Scotts Valley, CA 95067

Cover and Interior Design by Anne' Phillips, APGrafik Studio
http://facebook.com/ApGrafikStudio

ISBN-10: 0-9796589-1-8

ISBN-13: 978-0-9796589-1-4

Printed in the United States of America

To my family

Table of Contents

Introduction 9

Coming Out of the Age of Darkness and Into the Light (Or, The Word of God is the Universe) 20

How to Attain the Power of a Shaman and Fulfill Your Divine Purpose 51

What I Learned and What's Important to Know 89

What Will Happen in the Next Several Years 108

Questions and Answers 114

Thank You! 134

About the Author 135

The Spiritual Awakening Process

Coming Out of the Darkness and Into the Light

Introduction

This book is an update of my eBook titled, *Activating 2012: A Practical Guide for Navigating 2012 With Confidence and Clarity,* which I published in November of 2009. I updated it, gave it a new title, and am relaunching it because December 2012 has come and gone, yet many are still unaware of the significance of that date and what the end of the Mayan calendar actually signifies.

In fact, we can say that the true meaning of the 2012 time period (which has been referred to as the Great Shift in Consciousness, the galactic shift, the coming out of the Age of Darkness and into the Age of Light, the period of worldwide spiritual awakening) is still largely hidden from society. Which slows down the shift that's occurring.

Before December 2012, many teachers in the spiritual community speculated about the events that would transpire around that date. The Mayan Calendar would end on December 21, 2012 and many contemplated as to what the Mayans tried to communicate to us, the current residents of planet Earth, when they abruptly ended their calendar on this date, and what this ending signified for humanity's future.

I recall that beginning around the year 2008 or 2009, most everyone seemed to be interested in the 2012 shift. The Hollywood movie *2012*, which came out in the U.S and Canada on November 13th, 2009, was a disaster film in the old style of Atlantis about the end of time.

Physicists, astronomers and other scientists were concerned about certain cosmic phenomena affecting our planet and solar system. Economists were concerned about the shifts in global economies. Visionaries and spiritual teachers spoke of a shift in consciousness that humanity is undergoing at this moment in time. The Ascension, the Great Shift, the Rapture, the dimensional shift, the Omega Point, as well as other terms, were used to describe what was occurring.

The topic of 2012 was no longer reserved for Mayans, Hopi Indians and those who channeled information from other realms, but was very much in the mainstream. Even Internet marketers discussed the implications of 2012 with keen interest.

It seemed that no aspect of our world would be left untouched by this powerful shift. So what happened with 2012? Have the promises of this Great Shift in Consciousness been fulfilled? Or can it be that we're really still very much on track? Are we *right now* experiencing the end of a long cosmic cycle that will take the Earth and its inhabitants into a much more harmonious state, a "Golden Age," a lasting peace as many have claimed?

In the early 2000s I attended a number of lectures given by a Catholic priest named Father Charlie Moore. A former district attorney for Santa Cruz County, California and a scholar of theology, language and history, Father Moore did not discuss the topic of 2012 *per se*, even though he spoke a great deal about the Age of Darkness and the coming Age of Light. Which was understandable, given that in the early 2000s, 2012 was a number of years off in the future and not yet high on people's radar. Furthermore, the astronomy of the 2012 alignment might not have been well known at the time.

However, Father Moore said he had learned a number of things from the Mayans in Central America, whom he had visited. He learned of their visions and prayers; he learned about the ways of the shaman. He said the Mayans brought shamanism back to Guatemala, back to the planet, around 1970. And back with him, he brought the following prayer:

"May the heart of the Earth flow to the heart of the Heavens through my heart and through all our hearts together, and may our hearts be the heart of every sentient being in all the Universe and may the heart of the heavens flow to the heart of the Earth through my heart, and through all our hearts together, and may our hearts be the heart of all Humankind."

Father Moore further stated that Moses was a shaman, and so was Jesus. He said the Jesus portrayed in the New Testament was not the real Jesus. In fact, the real Jesus proposed religious reform back to shamanism, which was a threat to the establishment and the ruling elite. Jesus rebelled against the Roman Empire and was a threat to the ruling elite because he wanted to bring the church (Judaism) and its followers back to its original roots—shamanism.

What's so special about shamanism and what do shamans do? For one thing, they're connected with the natural world, they have dream visions, and they follow their intuition. They have a strong relationship with the spirit world, they have a well-developed internal guidance system and they *follow* their inner guidance.

The shaman's world consists of a spiritual world and a physical world. Their spiritual world includes their dreams, their spiritual guides and their inner guidance. Their physical world includes their sensory perception, their vision, awareness, consciousness and body. And in a shaman, these two levels happen to be well integrated.

So when shamans walk down the street and they don't know which direction to go, for example, the input from the physical world and the input from the spiritual world marries inside of them so that when they move, they're moving in the physical world as a result of the spiritual world. It's the integrating of these two levels of experience that they do pretty much automatically that allows a third level to be born within them—their soul expressing itself in the world.

Father Moore said that the Age of Darkness corresponds to the time when we've forgotten how to use our intuition, our internal powers, and the coming Age of Light corresponds to the time when we begin to use our "equipment" (our left brain and right brain, both) fully again.

According to Father Moore, the Bible is not the Word of God, and neither is the Torah or the Koran. The Bible may have been originally inspired by true masters, by shamans, but over time the books of the Bible have undergone changes by those whose agenda was to spread the control of empire. Those books as they're written today are the workings of empire. The Word of God is not the Bible, the Word of God is the Universe, Father Moore taught.

Another of Father Moore's main messages pertained to the founding of our country, America. In almost every talk he gave (and I attended about half a dozen of them) he would point out that our country's dream vision—the American dream—was inspired by Native Americans, by the Iroquois nation, by shamans whose dream vision was "freedom, equality and brother / sisterhood."

This idea of freedom, equality and brother / sisterhood for America was adopted by Benjamin Franklin (a Quaker, whose philosophy was actually similar to that of the Iroquois nation) and Thomas Jefferson, who had gone to the Iroquois Indians for some of the inspiration for the writing of the Declaration of Independence. Our founding fathers knew they (the colonists from Europe) needed to imitate the Iroquois Indians—rather than the other way around.

And in fact, America has influenced Europe. According to Father Moore, the discovery of America and Native American culture changed Europe significantly. Through American influence, democracy was birthed in Europe.

Franklin and Jefferson had to fight like bearcats to get that dream vision into our country's founding documents. Unfortunately, it didn't take long for Alexander Hamilton, the agent for the European banks (the founders of Wall Street), to shoot it down.

As we well know, Alexander Hamilton and the European banks he represented had a different ideology for the United States of America. According to the European banks, which later became Wall Street, greed is a virtue, murder is not a crime, and the end justifies the means.

Here's a really good, current example of this Wall Street insanity. As I'm updating this book, a historic gathering of native tribes and their supporters, including American veterans, are standing with the Standing Rock Sioux Indians, in protest of the Dakota Access Pipeline that is to run through the Sioux Indian reservation. Crude oil is to be piped down to the Gulf Coast for refining, then shipped by tankers to China. (Yes, you read that right. To China.) Which will result in a nice profit for a few. Nothing matters except for this profit. Your reservation, the Missouri River, the groundwater and the environment be damned.

I've been following raw food guru David Wolfe, who was at the Standing Rock Reservation to stand against not only Big Oil, Big Banks and greed, but against catastrophic ways of life, the corruption of the human spirit, fake science (like myself, David Wolfe has a degree in engineering), and evil itself. (For an incredible, eye-witness perspective on the Standing Rock conflict as well as an eye-opening, informative account with interviewer Lucien Gauthier, google "David Wolfe Standing Rock.")

But getting back to our country's founding principles ... Our nation's motto can be found on the Great Seal of the United States. It's been there since the Founding Fathers, placed there by Thomas Jefferson, said Father Moore. And according to Father Moore's interpretation of the original, Latin version, the motto says as follows: "The Divinity nods with consent and approval upon the things we have begun, a renewal of the ancient order of affairs, that out of many should be one, in order that in one another, and the Divinity, we may forever trust."

Like the Bible, the motto of our nation has been altered and distorted over time. This is why Father Moore went back to the original, unaltered Latin version and personally interpreted it for our knowledge and benefit. And he emphasized the fact that America's original motto said *ancient* order of affairs, not *new* order of affairs. Meaning, the ancient world that Jesus Christ was working toward, to religious reform back to shamanism, to how things were before we were visited by, and manipulated by, the colonist-gods, our ruling elite, the founders of Empire.

Father Moore passed away in 2007 at the age of 80. If he were alive today he'd look at the state of this country and say that we've abandoned the American dream. He'd remind us that this is the reason why the rest of the world looks at the United States with contempt and disrespect. And he'd say that we must turn to the spirit of this land and get the American dream back.

Regarding our recently elected president, it really doesn't matter a whole lot who that is. Both Hillary and Donald would serve Big Business once in office, rather than having the public interest in mind. The truth is, regardless of who is president the American people have a lot of work to do, and a lot of transformation to go through in order to make this country "great again." And remember, the more challenging the situation, the greater the potential for faster transformation. (One thing for certain though is that we are done with the Clinton / Bush era and change is definitely on the horizon.)

We're going to have to wake up to the deeper truths, the hidden truths of our history. We're going to have to stand up and fight like bearcats for what we believe in. Not necessarily fight like getting ourselves into physical fights, but fight like finally waking up to the power that's dormant within us, letting our voices be heard and known, drawing lines in the sand, making lifestyle changes that increase our health, and voting with our dollars. No more sitting on the sidelines.

Most things you hear about in the news or on the Internet you can't do anything about anyway, but you do need to focus your efforts on what *you* need to do, on your *higher life purpose* (your divine purpose)—by becoming the best possible shaman you can be, the best possible version of yourself. (Yes, the power of a shaman—Christ Consciousness—is dormant within you.)

I wish Father Charlie Moore were still with us, educating us with his vast knowledge and wisdom. But since he isn't, I'm honoring his legacy and his memory by sharing things I've learned when I heard him speak in the 2000s.

The Purpose of this Book

The purpose of this book is not to expound on the points made above as that's not my area of expertise. Readers who are interested in the hidden truths of human history are referred to Father Charlie Moore's book titled, *Synthesis Remembered: Awakening Original Innocence,* as well as the more than 50 books listed in the back of that book for further reference. Father Moore's hardcover book *Synthesis Remembered* was published in December of 2006 by Mooredune Publications and is available on Amazon. (A year after his book was published, he passed away.)

There are also a number of radio interviews of Father Moore that you can access online by typing "Father Charlie Moore" into the Google search engine. For old-schoolers, cassette tapes of his talks can still be purchased online as well.

Rather, the purpose of this book is twofold: One, to discuss in concrete terms what this Great Shift / Coming out of the Dark Ages (the "Bigger Picture") is about and two, to provide you with the tools you need to activate your own shift in consciousness and awaken the powers of a shaman in you. (As Father Moore would say, to help you hear the whispers of your heart and use your "equipment" fully again.) So that you become the master of your life and fulfill your higher life purpose.

Yes, you—a shaman. Which is what we need to become in order to restore this country to a true democracy—and what our Founding Fathers Benjamin Franklin and Thomas Jefferson originally intended. It's what Jesus Christ taught his followers, the followers of "The Way;" it's the return to Christ Consciousness.

The latter is a process, an unfolding that begins with reconnecting to your "higher self," your "higher consciousness," or as Father Moore put it, your heart-mind. You may call this process "connecting to Christ consciousness," if you like. Because that's what this is.

When you connect within, you'll experience what's written in the Gospel of Thomas. Not "seek and ye shall find" as that's a commandment and masters never give commandments, Father Charlie Moore writes in his book, but it's more like the following:

"Those who seek will find, and that is a promise. Those who find, will find the truth in their own heart. And those who find that truth will be disturbed because of the conflict between what their heart tells them and what they are being told by others.

"Those who are disturbed will wonder and ponder, and at last they will choose the truth in their own heart. They will then become masters of themselves and become truly human, which is the best thing any human can be."—from *Synthesis Remembered: Awakening Original Innocence*.

We are on the edge of tumultuous change on this planet. It is my intention that this book you hold in your hands comforts you, spares you a ton of pain, and assists you in your spiritual awakening process, which is actually twofold: one, awakening to your individual spiritual journey and fulfilling your divine purpose and two, awakening to humanity's collective spiritual journey (the "Bigger Picture").

Awakening to the Bigger Picture (the Great Shift in Consciousness, and galactic awareness) is extremely important because doing so will help you fulfill your divine purpose. And likewise, the more you become a shaman and fulfill your divine purpose, the more you'll awaken to and understand the Bigger Picture, our collective spiritual journey. I wish you and yours much success on your spiritual path.

Coming Out of the Age of Darkness and Into the Light (Or, The Word of God is the Universe)

This chapter gives some background information helpful to understanding what's currently happening in the world regarding the shift from one age to another, and why so much is occurring at this moment in time.

Some physicists and astronomers are focusing on understanding the physical events occurring at the planetary and solar system level and it's worthwhile for the average person to be aware of these phenomena. For example, I've read about the relatively recent changes to the Earth's icecaps and overall shape, increased solar magnetics, gravitational waves and activity, the melting of the icecaps on the planet Mars, and magnetic and polar shifts in the other planets of our solar system. The changes appear to be solar system wide, but we have not heard much from scientists as to why these phenomena may be occurring right now.

Back in the summer of 2009, when I did the research for this chapter, I also read information from channeled sources that stated that on December 21, 2012, our Sun would align with the Galactic Center, or what's referred to as the "Galactic Sun." The Galactic Center may be considered the "Sun" of our Sun.

(Interestingly, the source of this channeled information supposedly from the "other realm" claimed to be a member of the "Galactic Federation.")

I asked a friend who's an amateur astrologer to explain to me what "aligning with the Galactic Center" actually meant. He said that because of the Earth's wobble, the Earth goes through an approximately 26,000-year cycle called the "Precession of the Equinoxes" and that the ecliptics of these systems would be aligned on December 21, 2012.

Back then, I spent a few days on the Internet trying to understand what all this meant and discovered a lot of confusion about the exact nature of this alignment (which is understandable, given its complexity). So then I reached out to the Cornell University alumni network asking for a professional or amateur astronomer to help explain this geometry to me, and received some interesting responses. Basically, I was told that nothing was happening and don't worry about anything. (I wasn't worried, I just wanted to understand exactly the relationships of this alignment.)

I researched the Internet further and discovered that on December 21, 2012 the center of the Earth, the center of the Sun and the Galactic equator are not uniquely aligned as you might expect of collinear points on a line. In fact, our solar system is currently nowhere near the galactic equator but is far north of the equatorial plane of the Milky Way. (Our solar system lies about 20 light-years above the plane of the galaxy, according to an article by Nola Taylor Redd on Space.com.)

Rather, what I discovered on a European university's astronomy institute website (the Astronomical Institute at Utrecht

University in the Netherlands) is that around the time of 2012, a rare astronomical conjunction is occurring that happens once every 25,800 or so years—the conjunction of the winter solstice sun and the centerline (equator) of the Milky Way galaxy.

This is because of the fact that, besides the commonly known rotation-on-axis motion that one Earth day makes (daily rotation) and the orbit-around-the-Sun motion that one Earth year makes (annual revolution), the Earth makes a third circular path around the sky called the precession of the equinoxes, which takes about 25,800 years to complete. Interestingly, the precession of the equinoxes is related to the zodiac and determines the astrological ages. Every 2160 years or thereabouts, the Earth moves into a new sign of the zodiac, and the 12 signs of the zodiac make up one precession cycle.

An interesting side note: modern astronomers, both professional and amateur, use the zodiac as a guide to find celestial objects in the night sky. And recent evidence from an archeological dig in Turkey conducted by German archeologists dates the zodiac to about 10,000 BCE. (Does this make you wonder ... at least a little bit?)

This path of the Earth around the night sky is also called the Earth's "wobble" and is a result of the Earth being off its axis. (Currently, the Earth's North Pole points to the North Star—also called Polaris—but this gradually changes with the precession cycle.)

I was thrilled to see that someone at an institute of higher learning had the generosity and the patience to share scientific information about this conjunction with the public and to discuss its implications, rather than disregarding it or calling it a hoax, making it seem as though nothing unique at all was happening at this point in time, or assuming the public simply wanted to know if any "special effects in the sky" were visible on that date so that we could make informed decisions about where to pull up a chair, or whether it was a good idea to build an underground shelter, or not. But before I discuss the details of the conjunction, I want to say a little more about what I learned about the Mayan Long Count Calendar (the one that ended on December 21, 2012.)

The Mayan long count calendar is in the form of a circle (it's cyclic rather than linear like our modern calendar) and one cycle happens to be about 25,625 years—which is close to the length of time it takes to complete one precession of the equinoxes, or one cycle of the zodiac around the night sky. (A small discrepancy in the numbers is allowed as over the centuries, the time it took the Earth to physically complete one precession has varied slightly.) This suggests that we are leaving behind an old cycle and entering a new one, rather than it being the "end of times."

Have the Mayans planned their calendar to be associated with the precession of the equinoxes and have they designed the end date of this calendar to correspond with a rare astronomical alignment? Is this a coincidence, or were the ancient Mayans trying to tell us modern humans something about our history? Or maybe something about the level and sophistication of their technology and / or knowledge?

Now some astronomers assert that this conjunction has already occurred on December 21, 1998 and if you use the centerline (equator) of the galaxy defined by the IAU (International Astronomical Union), it already has. But the Milky Way galaxy has no clear definition or boundaries. It has an amorphous shape much like an amoeba that's not so easily bisected. Furthermore, *not all astronomers* agree that the centerline selected by the IAU is the best one.

In any case, moving the centerline up or down by one half of one degree results in an error in the conjunction timeline of plus or minus 36 years. According to the Astronomical Institute at Utrecht University the Milky Way is, on average, about 12 degrees wide in the night sky, and a shift of one-half of one degree in the centerline would give us a 2034 end date.

However, another source, an article in the *Scientific American*, says the ragged, hazy band of light that is the Milky Way is about 15 degrees wide in the night sky ... showing us that a small error in the currently established centerline is not only possible, it's highly likely.

If we move the centerline less than one quarter of one degree from the current line established by the IAU, we would have a December 21, 2012 end date. This means, at least to me, that the Mayan calendar end date quite accurately coincides with a rare astronomical alignment that happens to symbolize a "crossroads," the beginning of a new era. So, what we have here is a conjunction that's real, that happens twice in a 26,000-year precession cycle (once every 13,000 years), and it is happening pretty much without the public's awareness.

Furthermore, another factor not addressed by the Astronomical Institute at Utrecht University introduces yet another small error in the conjunction timeline. This small potential error has to do with a 41,000-year cycle in the Earth's axial tilt where Earth's axis varies from an angle of 21.5 to 24.5 degrees. Currently, the Earth's axial tilt is about 23.5 degrees.

An interesting side note: The Earth being off its axis by a significant angle is the reason why we have the "duality of the seasons"—the hot, hot summers and the cold, cold winters.

What does all this mean? It means our astronomers can easily be off by a few years in the conjunction timeline. Perhaps the Mayans were more accurate than modern astronomers? Or perhaps it's the Mayans who were off by a few years? But really, does being off by a few years in a 26,000-year cycle matter?

This led me to ask—what did the Mayans know (that we discovered only recently) and how did they know it? Because apparently, the Mayan Long Count Calendar was established around the year 355 BCE.

Some scholars have argued that the Mayan calendar does not predict what was to happen on December 21, 2012 and they're right about that—but that's not what I found interesting. What I found interesting is that many years before the birth of Christ, the Mayans were aware of an astronomical cycle the Earth and our solar system makes with respect to the Milky Way Galaxy that we had no idea about ... until just recently.

Why did the Mayans deem it important to track this galactic cycle and document it in their records for us to discover and contemplate? Why did they choose an end date to their calendar that corresponds to a rare astronomical conjunction? What were they trying to tell us?

I learned in school that Copernicus was the first to demonstrate, using scientific modeling, that the Sun was at the center of the solar system and that it was the Earth that revolved around the Sun. Before Copernicus, the authorities proclaimed that the Sun revolved around the Earth and the Earth stood still at the center of the Universe. Copernicus published his book in 1543 and is regarded as the father of both modern astronomy and the scientific revolution. I also learned in school that the Church was threatened when Copernicus brought forth this new understanding and that he was excommunicated from the Church for spreading this heresy.

The explanation that the Mayans were "careful observers" of the night sky does not fly with me—it takes hundreds of years to see a noticeable change in the position of the stars in the night sky. The indigenous Mayans definitely were "connected to the Earth," but that doesn't explain their knowledge of galactic cycles. How do you observe something that happens once every 13,000 years?

Certainly, the Mayans did not attain this knowledge by hallucinating on wild mushrooms or even the careful observation (maybe with binoculars?) of a remote astronomical event that happens once every 13,000 years. Remember that Copernicus observed a common event that not only happens every single year (the length of time it takes the Earth to complete one cycle around the Sun) but the repeating cycles of the seasons assisted us in observing it.

Furthermore, the website of this European astronomical institute clearly states that the conjunction is *not visible from Earth*, because the Sun would be in the "solsticial point" and the solsticial point is above the horizon only during the day (i.e. you can't see the night sky during the day). I suppose the astronomers are implying here that the conjunction is only visible from locations outside the Earth—the moon, say, or maybe Venus or Mars.

Furthermore, the lines in the sky are imaginary, not visible. For example, you can take the center of the Earth and the center of the Sun and connect the two points with an imaginary line, but that line would not be visible.

For this engineer, anyway, there are only two possible explanations to the Mayan questions—either the Mayans had the knowledge and the technology to make not only precise solar system measurements but also galactic system measurements almost 1,900 years before Copernicus, or else they must have inherited this information and knowledge (and perhaps technology?) from other beings who had it.

However, the scientific consensus at the time of my research seemed to be that it is a *coincidence* that the Mayan Long Count Calendar equals the length of time it takes for one precession cycle (one zodiac cycle) to occur and that it is yet *another* coincidence that the end of this calendar happens to correspond to a rare astronomical conjunction. But what happens when you don't believe in coincidence? Then the scientific explanation becomes a problem.

Some scientists deny that the Mayans could have known what the evidence plainly shows they knew simply because it doesn't fit into the current scientific and historic paradigm. They can't seem to reconcile the new information with what was taught at University about ancient peoples and human history. That's why so far, the coincidence explanation is the best they have. (And at the end of 2016, when I'm updating this book, not much seems to have changed since I wrote the first version.)

Pre-2012, "let's not panic the panicky public" may have been an evasive tactic used to divert attention away from the fact that scientists did not have satisfactory explanations—at least none they wanted to share with the public. Of course, pre-2012 they also wanted to prevent mass fear surrounding the doom and gloom predictions of collisions with asteroids, encounters with massive solar flares, or a serious heating up of the planet. (Even as Hollywood, and some shady websites, prepared to scare the heck out of you.)

Here is what I wanted to know: 13,000 years ago, the last time an alignment with the galactic centerline occurred, did our ancestors do the calculations and plot out this event on paper, in the sand, or on cave walls, seeing that according to scholars of history, paper was first invented in China in the 2nd century CE? And when did we (modern humans) first become aware of this alignment? Here's one more thing I'd like to know: Did anything significant happen around 13,000 years ago?

Although some critics are opposed to the proposal that civilizations possessing superior technology existed in the Earth's past, how else can we explain the Mayan phenomena using logic and reasoning? Especially since this hypothesis would help us explain some events in human history that currently make little sense. (For example, the building of pyramids all around the planet.)

Another interesting cultural symbol that's been associated with the precession of the equinoxes for ages—although relatively few are aware of this association—is the solar cross. The cross in a circle happens to be an ancient symbol, an astronomical as well as astrological symbol for the planet Earth, and a spiritual symbol used in many cultures.

The solar cross is also known as the zodiac cross, the Celtic cross, the heavenly cross (the cross that's found in the heavens), or simply the holy cross. Variations of this cross have been seen in prehistoric petroglyphs, including in Mayan and Egyptian drawings and artifacts.

The solar cross symbol also shows up almost everywhere in modern culture: in churches and graveyards, on jewelry and automobiles, and even as permanent marks on the human body in the form of tattoos. It's worth your while to go to Google Images, type in "solar cross" and examine the images that come up. A simple illustration of the solar cross is shown below.

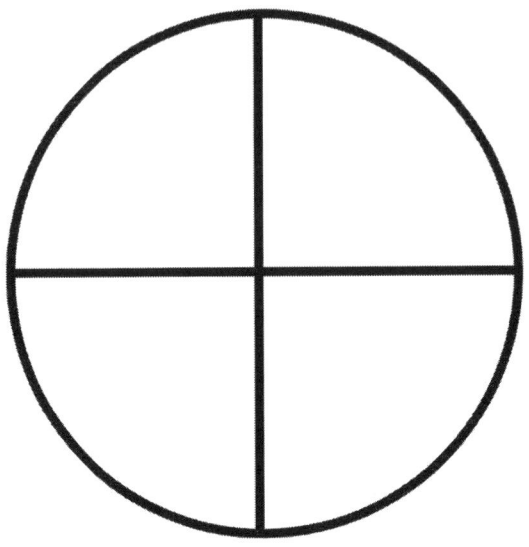

The Solar Cross

I usually don't consult astrology for guidance on daily life and I don't know a whole lot about it, but I'm including a discussion of an aspect of it here because I found the symbolism and metaphors positively eye-opening. My background is in materials science and engineering (I graduated with a bachelor's degree from Cornell University's engineering school in 1983) and I'm well aware that the structure of a material on a microscopic level (e.g. the alignment of its atoms) affects the material's behavior and properties on a macroscopic level. I can see the parallel between cosmic bodies (the macrocosm) and that they can affect our bodies (the microcosm). In fact, this is yet another way of saying, as above, so below.

Astrology may simply be viewed as a symbolic interpretation of astronomy. Because of my many helpful personal experiences involving symbolism and metaphor, a few of which I'll share later in this book, I'm aware that metaphor is one way the higher self ("higher consciousness") communicates with "lower consciousness" (our awareness). I also assert that it's essential that we become "symbol-literate," especially at this time of great change. Now, getting back to understanding the alignment that's occurring at this point in time …

We can look at the Earth's precession cycle (the circular movement of the Earth's axis through the various constellations in the sky) as a sacred geometry representing cyclical global change. We can make a simple model of the Earth's precession cycle where the circle below represents the movement of the Earth's North Pole axis over the 26,000-year cycle. (The Earth's axis moves clockwise on the circle.) We can put a horizontal line through the circle's center that represents the unmoving galactic equatorial plane (it remains essentially unmoving over the period of the cycle). We can shade the bottom half to represent the dark; the top half will represent the light. I have labeled points on this circle to represent where we are at this moment in the precession cycle. In the 26,000-year timeline, we are currently at point D.

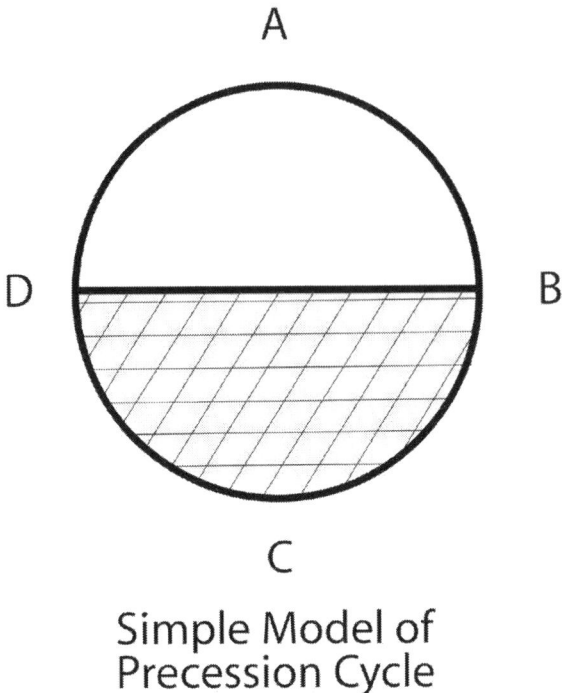

Simple Model of Precession Cycle

Astrologers typically plot the moving vernal axis (the spring equinox point) and the unmoving galactic equatorial plane. (The vernal axis is always 90 degrees clockwise from the polar axis, and the polar axis can be viewed as a point on the circle that represents where we are in the precession cycle.) We are interested in the relationship between Earth's moving north pole and the fixed galactic plane because it provides insight into Earth's precessional cycle and the collective evolution cycle of the souls manifested on Earth.

So what this means is that when we're at position D (when the North Pole points to position D—which is now), the vernal axis ("VA") makes a vertical line (that points to position A on the circle) through the center point of the circle and a cross is formed between the vertical vernal axis and the fixed horizontal galactic axis ("GA").

Astronomically, this means that there's an imaginary cross in the sky and metaphorically, that we are currently at a "crossroads." (See the illustration below.)

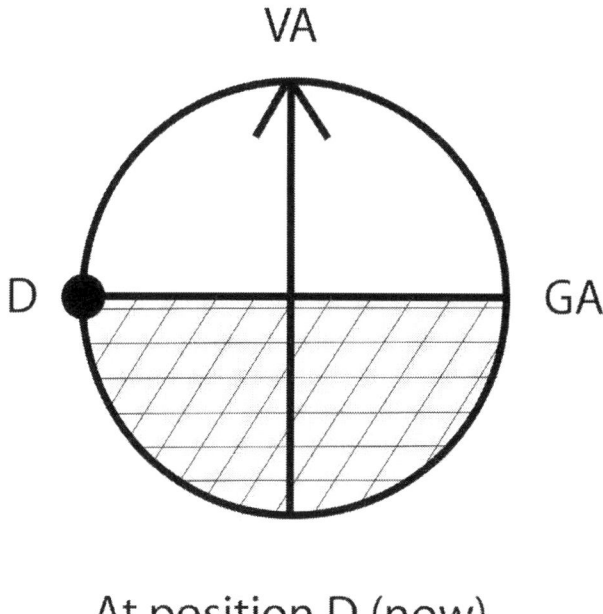

At position D (now)

At this point, the North Pole begins to lean *toward* the galactic plane where there is greater galactic light, in other words toward the center of the Milky Way galaxy where the galactic core is, rather than pointing away from the galactic core and toward the outer areas of the galaxy. This symbolizes the beginning of the "summer" half of the precession cycle and the Earth beginning to reorient itself to, to "re-tune" itself to, galactic awareness / consciousness.

Another interesting side note: According to astrologers, position D is the location of the galactic equatorial node called the "Gate of Man," while position B is the location of the galactic equatorial node called the "Gate of God." This means the Earth's North Pole is currently on the Gate of Man and the vernal axis is flipping toward the Gate of God.

To see a 3-dimensional representation of the relationships between the galactic equatorial plane, the North Pole, the vernal axis, the constellations of the zodiac, the "Gate of God" and the "Gate of Man" and to further study these relationships, visit Nick Anthony Fiorenza's website, where I found most of this information. Nick's website address is: Lunarplanner.com/HolyCross.html. He even has a video on that page showing the relationships over the 26,000-year cycle. (However, it isn't necessary to understand the complex geometric relationships to follow along in this book as I have simplified the concepts.)

So ... when the Earth's North Pole points to position A in the precession cycle (which will happen approximately 6500 years from now—see the illustration labeled "Simple Model of Precession Cycle"), the vernal axis is aligned with the horizontal galactic equatorial axis (i.e. there is no cross), and the polar axis is nearly parallel with the plane of the galaxy (it is fully in the light of the galactic plane, or fully in "galactic light" or "galactic consciousness"). At that point in time, the vernal axis points to the "Gate of God"—the primary galactic equatorial node that's closest to Galactic Center. (Galactic Center can be viewed as the "Sun" of our Sun. Galactic Center is a Black Hole in the center of the Milky Way Galaxy. In other words, our Sun's "Sun" is a Black Hole.) This is the most illumined position of the entire precession cycle. For 3D and 4D visuals of these celestial relationships, see Nick Anthony Fiorenza's website at the address on page 34.

When the Earth's North Pole points to position B (which happened approximately 13,000 years ago and will happen again in 13,000 years), the polar axis is parallel to the galactic plane and the vernal axis is perpendicular and pointing down. Here we have another cross in the sky, another crossroads. At this point the North Pole begins to lean *away from* galactic light (symbolizing the beginning of the "winter" half of the precession cycle and a fall in galactic awareness).

When the Earth's North Pole points to position C (which happened about 6,500 years ago), the polar axis is tilted *farthest away* from the plane of the galaxy (furthest away from galactic light or consciousness, symbolizing the "darkest point" in humanity's consciousness). The vernal axis is parallel and reversed with the galactic plane (i.e. there is no cross, or crossroads) and the vernal axis points to the "Gate of Man"—the primary galactic equatorial node that is farthest away from Galactic Center.

Although visualizing all the celestial relationships and understanding the astronomical details can be quite a challenge, the symbolic relationships are important enough to include here. It's not necessary to understand the astronomical and astrological details to get the important concepts in this book. I included these concepts in simplified from to give you a basic understanding of what the solar cross may have represented to ancient peoples, and so that you can familiarize yourself with the symbolism within it.

If you'd like to study the astronomical and astrological details more closely, there are many sources on the Internet besides the one mentioned above. There's also an organization called The Binary Research Institute. The Binary Research Institute holds an annual conference for scholars called CPAK—Conference on Precession and Ancient Knowledge. Their website has valuable information for those interested in further scientific and historical study of this material. CPAK had their 10th conference at the end of September of 2016 in Rancho Mirage, California.

Anyway ... the astronomical evidence suggests that we are at a critical point (a "crossroads") in humanity's history right now. That we're going through a global transition, a paradigm shift in our beliefs and awareness (personal as well as collective), is not a secret, at least not anymore.

The celestial alignment we are currently experiencing can be viewed as a huge catalyst for transformation and change on Earth. We are at the beginning of a period of greater light and awareness, the beginning of a "summer" in humanity's evolution. What this means is that humanity is headed toward the alignment of our selves or "egos" (our minds, our identities) with our "centers," our "cores"—our "higher selves" (the gateway, the bridge to the larger universe, our direct access to "God").

However, I feel there's something new happening this time around and that this is *not just another* 26,000-year cycle. We were not meant to go from periods of relative light to relative dark *ad infinitum*. This "new thing" has to do with the ending of the light / dark experience, the ending of duality. Perhaps this is what the Mayans were trying to tell us with the ending of their calendar on December 21, 2012—that we are in for a new kind of experience. Indeed, the idea of a "graduation" from the "wheel of karma" has been surfacing in the collective consciousness for some time now, although as usual, there are lots of interpretations as to what that actually means.

My understanding is that by aligning with one's higher self, there will be a retuning and an integration of the ego and the higher self. I view the "Gate of Man" as the ego (lower level consciousness, worldly consciousness) and the "Gate of God" as the higher self (higher level, bigger picture consciousness). I've discovered that the higher self is the gateway to God, to the larger universe. I've also found that when you "align" with your higher self, when you strengthen the relationship with your soul / higher self, this will over time lead to the integration of your higher self with your ego and the raising of your consciousness. Strengthening the relationship with your higher self leads to the beginning of awakening and to becoming a master of your life, a shaman. On a collective level, it marks the end of duality, the end of the cycle of light and dark.

I don't agree with the view that the ego needs to be "undone," "negated," or "at least brought down a peg or two." This is lower-level consciousness thinking and shows a lack of true understanding of the purpose behind humanity's time in duality. (I'll explain further in a later chapter.)

With regard to the bigger picture, it wouldn't surprise me if the Mayan calendar's end date of December 21, 2012 also marked another important alignment—the alignment of our Milky Way Galaxy with the center of the Cosmos. Although I certainly cannot prove that this larger alignment is occurring, my intuitive sense is that not only our planet and solar system are undergoing a unique transformation at this time, but our entire galaxy as well. (The same galaxy that I seem to recall from childhood as being "out in some forgotten corner of the universe". . .)

All life is based upon cycles, and this life is affected by the placement of planets and stars, including their relationship to Galactic Center as well as to Cosmic Center. Although astronomical events do affect what happens on this planet, this isn't my area of expertise. I simply have pointed out some unanswered questions and interesting observations that seem to validate that change in our consciousness is imminent. Luckily, there's an abundance of quality information in books and on the Internet that address these scientific and historical topics. You may wish to read up on some of these topics to satisfy your own curiosity.

As we well know, the extent to which we can influence astronomical events is minimal and that it's much better to work on the things you can change—for instance, the alignment of your mind (thoughts and beliefs) and body (actions) with your higher self (which is itself aligned with the divine plan). There is a way to get in harmony with divine plan which doesn't require the study of astronomy or astrology. For our purposes, it's enough to be aware that there's a certain order and sequence to the unfolding of life in the cosmos and that this order does influence what we experience on our planet.

The more important topic (and the focus of this book) is: How do we strengthen the relationship with our higher self and raise our awareness? How do we activate a shift in our consciousness and awakening so that we hold the power of a shaman in our hearts? How do we become masters of our lives and make a positive difference in the world? (Just as America's Founding Fathers—and Father Charlie Moore—had intended.)

You might also wonder what happened to us that we experienced a "fall in consciousness" about 13,000 years ago. Does this fall in consciousness correspond to the fall hinted at in the Old Testament, the banishment from the Garden of Eden? Or does it correspond to the fall of Atlantis?

If there indeed were a fall in consciousness then the cure to this fall seems to be the shift in consciousness that we're beginning to experience at this time. Perhaps it's time we stop ignoring or fearing the upcoming changes but empower ourselves by consciously activating the shift within us. In other words, become the shaman and be the change you want to see in the world. Although many people are in crisis at this time, the crises help activate the transformation and the shift in consciousness within us.

Later in this book I'll explain why the "fall in consciousness" was not a bad thing and that it was something that was divinely inspired with our best and highest interests in mind. But first, our focus will be on activating this shift in consciousness within us, because it's much more likely that we'll accept the idea of a divine planning of "going through the dark" after we make that shift in consciousness, after we actually become empowered enough that we can see a successful resolution to our own crises.

By now you may be wondering what makes me qualified to write about the changes that we will undergo during this time of "great shift in consciousness"—if you're even convinced there will be any changes. Besides the grappling of scientists for explanations as to what is occurring and the dogma of various religions, there also exists information that is "channeled." This is when a person with an ability to go into an altered state of consciousness channels a voice considered from a higher realm.

Often the voice says things the person who's doing the channeling has no way of knowing in his or her normal state of awareness. Sometimes, the person being the vehicle for the information being channeled is not conscious of what he or she is saying during the channeling, i.e., she does not remember what she said. (This, by the way, has been used as an argument and validation that the information must be more valid or superior to "normal state" information. Because it did not come from normal human awareness, the logic goes, it must be more valid somehow. But of course, all types of information must be questioned and tested for validity, accuracy and consistency.)

During the last decade or two, there's been a lot of channeled information about the shift in consciousness, 2012, and humanity's spiritual awakening on the Internet. Much of the information seems to be generally consistent (i.e. humanity is going through a number of internal and external changes, a process of spiritual evolution and awakening, a shift in "vibration"), but differences and vagueness in the details of how this awakening will actually occur remain.

I do not channel per se, such as I've witnessed some mediums be able to do ... to go on and for a half hour or even an hour. However, from approximately February 2001 through June 2005 I had information that turned out to be vital and instrumental to discovering my higher purpose channeled for me from beings in another realm who happened to call themselves the Counsel of Light. I believe the members of the Counsel of Light have had previous experience / lifetimes in this realm. Their purpose at this time is to help guide humanity in our personal and planetary shift.

The information from the Counsel of Light came to me through a gifted medium and teacher named Flo Aeveia Magdalena. Google "Soul Support Systems" to find out more about Flo's mission and organization.

The Counsel of Light is often spelled Council of Light. I've seen both spellings used in the literature. When I had to choose a spelling, I contemplated it for some time and finally chose "Counsel of Light." This is because "counsel" implies lawyer or "law-yer"—and I feel the Counsel of Light had something to do with the fundamental laws of the universe. However, it doesn't matter if it's spelled "Counsel" or "Council" as they are one and the same.

I do not believe the Counsel of Light (nor Esther Hick's well-known "Abraham" entity) know everything there is to know; I believe they are learning through us just as we learn from them. All are learning and evolving. There is a larger Divine Plan they and others can access and "read," but not everything is set in stone. An element of surprise is always present.

My sense is that we are currently going through a process that hasn't necessarily happened before—anywhere. Although *similar* events may have happened before elsewhere, I believe there's an element to this process humanity is going through right now that is somehow *completely new*—and that after this cycle of transformation, the Universe will never be the same again.

The Counsel of Light informed me in the early 2000s that I'd go through a particular process, and once I became familiar enough with the process I'd be able to teach it to others. They did not tell me then that it would be "the great shift in consciousness," but that's because they did not simply hand over to me what I needed to figure out for myself. They expected me to do my part of the deal, to reconnect to that part of myself that had direct access to God, to the divine plan and from there, to remember, to put things together, to figure things out, and then to offer this new understanding to the world. After all, how can you effectively teach a process to others that you did not in every important aspect go through yourself?

I also feel that the point of this "Great Shift" in consciousness is not so that each of us go into altered states of consciousness to channel entities from other realms. That would be strange. Rather, the point of this shift is to strengthen the relationship with your higher self so that this relationship is as real and as important to you as any of your other relationships, and to get in touch with the wisdom you've been accumulating since the beginning of time, including a higher-level understanding of our experience here on Earth as well as a higher-level understanding of your own life and evolutionary journey. (In other words, you becoming a shaman.)

This means that the wisdom and understanding of your higher self (your soul) with regard to your life and evolutionary journey is "transferred" little by little to your conscious mind. Gaining a higher-level understanding of your evolutionary journey will definitely shift your consciousness. It's what happened to me, and it's what's happening to many during this time of great change.

In fact, there's nothing all that new about channeling. People have channeled since Biblical times, at times claiming their channeling to be the inspired words of God. (Even today, there are people who claim to channel God.) Rather, what we can consider new is the integration that's occurring at this time: the integration of the spiritual (sometimes referred to as higher-level consciousness) with the physical (the 3rd dimension, or lower-level consciousness.)

Because this "Great Shift" has elements of the spiritual, the mystical and the unknown, there's been an unspoken assumption that information on it that's channeled is superior to information from human seekers grappling with present reality. But what if you were to combine both? In other words, the seeker / scientist applied the channeled information to her present reality, tested and experimented and pressed through the process of reconnecting with her higher self and shifting her consciousness, and kept track of what was happening and what was important during the process? Would that not be worth doing? After all, much of the channeled information has been telling us that we on this planet are doing something that *hasn't been done before*—shifting our consciousness from "normal consciousness" (i.e. "lower consciousness" or "fallen consciousness") to include our soul's consciousness while still in our physical body. In other words, we're ascending in our consciousness without having to die first.

Beings in the "other realms" might not know what shifting your consciousness while still in the physical body is like—which could be one reason why they say they're observing us with intense interest. Jesus Christ ascended in consciousness while still in his physical body, but this time it's part of Divine Plan that all of humanity follow his path. Christ himself even stated that we will be able to do what he did, and much more. (As Father Charlie Moore stated, Christ was a shaman with highly developed powers of telepathy.) This is why many spiritual teachers refer to this shift in consciousness as "finding the Christ consciousness within."

The details of my own process of awakening are found in my first book, the hardcover version titled, *What Everyone Believed: A Memoir of Intuition and Awakening*, and the Kindle version titled, *Reconnected: A Spiritual Awakening Memoir*, both available from Amazon.

In that book I share my personal story. I describe the process of reconnecting with my higher self (the gateway or bridge to higher consciousness, or Source), including the crises that catalyzed me to look within, and to question my beliefs about life and my life purpose. I describe my conversations with the Counsel of Light and what they told me, including the things they said were important for the process of awakening. I describe the amazing events and synchronicities that occurred once I mustered up the courage to go forward with my mission to be of service to humanity (even if I did not know at the time what that mission was, or that anything profound was going to happen after I took that scary plunge). And I describe the changes in my consciousness and my understanding of what we're doing on this planet, why we have been playing this crazy game called "duality" ("learning through contrast," learning through pain and suffering) and why so many things are changing at this time that are leading to the beginning of peace on this planet, the beginning of the end of suffering, the coming out of the age of darkness and into the light.

It's interesting that I had been searching for my life purpose for almost two decades, but it wasn't until I experienced a time of deep crisis that I was finally able to discover the details of what that purpose was. Because I knew (intuitively) that nothing or no one outside of myself could resolve my crises for me, I had no choice but to look within for the answers that would eventually come through my higher self ... which turned out to be the whole point. Reconnecting to my higher self, encouraging others to do the same, and teaching what I learned in the process is one of my main purposes here.

Many people are finding themselves in deep crises that they will not be able to resolve using the old methods—meaning anything that they already know. They will have to go within and look for the answers that come through their higher consciousness. But then again, that is the point.

I believe we're all going through that same process now, as part of the preparation for the end of this cycle of human experiencing. I believe we are shifting the human experience from one of "learning through pain" to one of "learning through joy." In the meantime, getting through the next few years will be the hardest thing we ever do as individuals and as a society. The next few years may be some of the toughest we ever experience—not necessarily physically but psychically (in terms of the spiritual, emotional, and mental growth that will be available to us if we so choose). The next few years will also be some of the most satisfying—if we muster up the courage to follow through with our intuition, inner guidance, and fulfill our part of the divine plan.

No one can tell you what to do. (Well, they'll say whatever they say, but you'll need to look within to evaluate what they say and find your own truth.) You will know what to do when you look within, when you reconnect within and learn to trust that knowing within. By following through with *your* higher life plan (your unique contribution to this important transformation), you will eventually attain an unprecedented level of success. Then you'll be able to look back with gratitude and appreciation for the experiences that transformed you (and for the people who have helped you along in your journey) . . . which sure sounds like the start of the "Golden Age" to me.

I believe that humanity *will* attain the Golden Age. There's no doubt about that in my mind. I say this because there were certain events and conditions that were "planted," "set up" in my life experience, to assure that I would actually go through with my higher life plan (the plan my higher self had agreed to before incarnating into this realm).

Your higher self knows you more than you know yourself, and your higher self knows how to get you to examine your life, change your mindset and take action that serves your highest good. Your higher self knows how to get your attention. Your higher self (your direct access to the divine) has "engineered" certain events in your life that will help you grow and transform.

Some of these events are crises that can be very painful. Many on the planet are going through a time of deep crisis right now. According to the Counsel of Light, I needed to experience the process of shifting my consciousness and keep track of the details of the process so that I can now offer a bigger picture understanding that will help people through this difficult time. A higher-level understanding of what's going on will reduce the fear and pain and help people move forward faster, and with more ease.

I can't do a thing about shifting the Earth's axes but I can teach people to focus on those things they can change—e.g. activate their own inner "polar" shift. (By this I mean a shift from limited consciousness to one that includes the consciousness of the higher self.) Indeed, visionaries and channels have stated that the "energy of consciousness" is being upgraded at this time—which to me means that we are shifting from a "limited consciousness" understanding of the life process to a higher-level understanding. When it comes to the changes in our solar system, we're just going along for the cosmic ride. But we can and will make changes in the human and societal systems on our planet and it will begin by evolving our consciousness on an individual level.

Back in November of 2009, when the movie *2012* first came out, I noticed something interesting in the preview. On the bottom of the "2012—Official Movie Site" web page (after you viewed the trailer) was a small image that said, "Farewell Atlantis." To the right of the image was a yellow sign in the shape of a diamond with the words "This is the end" on the sign.

Perhaps the visionaries who created this film are communicating that humanity is finally ready to say "farewell" to the entire experience that began with that fall. Perhaps the catastrophic fall of Atlantis many thousands of years ago corresponds to the fall in humanity's consciousness and level of awareness that happened as a result. And now that we've come to a certain point in our evolution, we are ready and able to expand our consciousness so that we can begin to remember and put the puzzle pieces together that will give us a much more complete, higher-level understanding of the human journey.

Before we go further, it's important to realize that while someone who has gone through the process I describe in this book can help by sharing her personal story and giving you some guidelines and helpful examples, you'll need to "step off the cliff" yourself. However, the more uncomfortable your life gets, the more you'll be inclined to take that next step and take that risk and leave behind your (not so comfortable) comfort zone. (I know this may sound harsh and I don't mean it to be, but I know that you might be going through some rough times at the moment and the rough times are exactly what motivated me to do what I needed to do.)

I understand that it may take a short while for you to "get up to speed" and to commit to the process outlined in the next chapter of this book. If this is the first time you're hearing or reading this kind of information, allow yourself some time to let it all sink in. However, there will quickly come a time when you will know that you need to take some kind of forward action. Once you do, it won't be long to see results that will help you continue on your path.

The following chapter will show you step by step what you need to be aware of and what you need to do to strengthen your relationship with your higher self (that part of you connected to divine plan, to All That Is, to the universe, to Interconnectedness, or if you prefer, to God). By strengthening the relationship with your higher self and following your inner guidance you'll become the master of your life, a shaman—and this is how you'll contribute your part to humanity coming out of the age of darkness and into the light.

I invite you to activate the shift in your consciousness so that you will discover your divine purpose, create extraordinary results from your soul, and become the best possible version of yourself—for yourself as well as for the greater good.

How to Attain the Power of a Shaman and Fulfill Your Divine Purpose

Although the details of your higher purpose will be unique to you (and will be revealed to you on a need-to-know basis through your higher self, which is your direct access to God and your part in the divine plan), the general process of strengthening the relationship with your higher self and reconnecting to that higher consciousness is basically the same for everyone.

Before I describe the various steps in the process, I'll share a bit about what others have said about what's required for you to "ascend" your consciousness or create a shift in your consciousness. Wynn Free (the author of *The Reincarnation of Edgar Cayce?*) has stated, "In order to participate in this new earth, your own heart chakra must be open slightly more than half or your energy field won't fit. So there's going to be a division of souls, those who graduate with the new earth and those who have to repeat the cycle of third chakra lessons."

Other teachers have endorsed this same idea, warning that the enlightening changes and transformation will not come easily unless one has an "open heart and an open mind." Furthermore, much of the information that's channeled stresses the importance of opening your heart and keeping it open and getting in touch with your intuition. Sometimes the importance of getting in touch with your higher self is mentioned as well. Still others say it's important to "acknowledge your Creator."

If Father Charlie Moore were alive today he'd advise us to "use the powers you were given," to get in touch with God through your heart, your higher self—the "holy spirit" part of you. In his talks, I heard Father Moore more than once say, "Instead of worshiping God, use the powers you were given! Be the glory of God. And help everyone else be the glory of God."

However, what does all this mean for your day-to-day life, exactly? What is the significance of having your heart chakra "open more than half?" How do you open your heart chakra? How do you "open your mind," "live your purpose," "sustain your vibration" or "unify your separation from Source?" General statements like "connect within," "follow your heart" and "use your intuition" might not be all that helpful. It just doesn't work to speak in generalities when it comes to these topics. It helps to have the tools, the detailed instructions for the "how-to," a number of real-life examples, and sometimes even the "why."

It's difficult to make these types of changes in your life if you don't have detailed descriptions of the process and real-life examples of what happened to others to which you can relate. Speaking in broad, vague and abstract concepts (including jargon) is okay, but only after a certain level of competence has been achieved.

Furthermore, I assert that what we're doing here on this planet is something new—ascending our consciousness without having to "give up" the physical body. If this really is new, then those who exist in the higher realms (from whom we've been receiving channeled information) would not have detailed descriptions of what we need to do and what it's going to be like in this dimension. How would they know when it hasn't happened yet? This earth experience is, after all, regarded as an experiment in soul evolution.

In fact, the culmination of this experiment (the end of this cycle and the beginning of what's new) is part of a collaborative effort between our realm and the higher realms, an integration of the physical and spiritual realms. This is why in order to supply the details of the process, someone in this realm had to use the information given her by those in the higher realm (in my case, the Counsel of Light), forge ahead as a pioneer (activating her intuition and shift in consciousness in the process), keep track of what she experienced and learned, what worked and what didn't work, and then put together what she learned in a comprehensive, easy-to-understand book.

In fact, I discovered there's much more to the reconnecting and awakening process than opening one's mind and that the words "keep an open heart and mind" do not do it justice. In this chapter, I'll provide you with the details of the process.

Since you're reading this book, you're probably a spiritual seeker and are aware that the human being consists of a body (the physical aspect of life) and a soul (the spiritual aspect, the part of ourselves that has been around forever). The human body can thus be viewed as a vehicle for the soul, a way the soul or the higher self can experience physicality, or life in the physical.

My understanding is that we are here on this planet to help each other learn, grow, evolve, love, appreciate, and come to know who we are and what we're truly capable of—which I like to summarize with the words "spiritual growth."

We accomplish this spiritual growth by helping make possible a wide variety of firsthand experiences for ourselves and others to live and learn through, including hardships and crises (those experiences that have the most potential for spiritual and emotional growth). We seek this spiritual growth because we know we cannot truly and completely appreciate the good in life until we have experienced the opposite first. We cannot really know what something is like (and develop compassion for ourselves and others) until we experience it ourselves. Helen Keller said it well: "Character cannot be developed in ease and quiet. Only through experience of trial and suffering can the soul be strengthened, ambition inspired, and success achieved."

We have been in this particular cycle of human experiencing for many thousands of years. (Although I'm sure we've been learning and evolving for much, much longer.) Some call this experience duality. In order for this incredible growth experience to have been possible, we've had to cut ourselves off from our higher consciousness (our connection to God, to the larger universe, to All That Is, to galactic light and consciousness.) We've had to cut ourselves off from knowing who we truly are and from where we came. The duality experience or "duality experiment" or "Earth Experiment" as it's sometimes called was an important part of the Divine Plan. Furthermore, it was sanctioned by the heavens, as we've seen in the previous chapter.

If we humans were consciously aware of the extent to which we (our higher selves) had planned this earth experience, I doubt we would have gone through with the plan. Like actors who know they wrote their ambitious script and then got lazy, we would have changed the script. However, in order to attain the highest level in our spiritual evolution (the fastest way being learning through pain and suffering), we had to forget. We chose to experience the fall in consciousness, to forget, for highly noble reasons—for the learning that comes from firsthand experiencing.

We knew this experience in duality would be temporary, a temporary sacrifice you might say, a mere blip on the radar screen of our entire existence. Our plan—the divine plan—was to "lose ourselves" in a physicality that repressed the spiritual and encouraged fear and separation and then, in struggle, to find our way back to Source again, having achieved an unprecedented level of growth and appreciation for who we are in the process. It is through adversity and struggle that we come to know and appreciate who we are, and who others are.

As we are now coming to the end of this cycle and becoming conscious of the bigger picture behind it, the higher perspective, what's happening is we are gradually transforming the learning process from one of learning through pain and suffering (through lower consciousness, "ego consciousness") to one of learning through joy (through the heart / soul). The timing for this development happens to be perfectly in line with heaven, as we've seen in the previous chapter. And what it requires of you is a shift in your consciousness, an integration of you, and for you to get in touch with the consciousness of your higher self. (Or as Father Moore would say, for you to get in touch with your heart.)

This does not mean your lower consciousness (your "ego") will be negated and neither do you need to "put it in its place" as if it's to blame for the conditions of your life. Your ego is not to blame. Your higher self is and always was in charge. Besides, you will still need your ego awareness to continue to exist on this planet. (And when you walk across the street, it is important to be aware of "3rd dimensional points of energy" such as cars, buses and trucks.)

What *will* be different when you begin the process of strengthening the relationship with your higher self and heart is this: Your higher self will begin to inform your 3rd dimensional experience more and more until you and your higher self are completely integrated and then you no longer think of your higher self as your "higher self" (or some mysterious or foreign aspect of you) but simply as "you." The more you integrate, the more wisdom you'll access, the more you'll understand, and the less of a mystery your higher self (or Oneness, or Interconnectedness, or synchronicity, or the shift in consciousness, or even your life story) will become.

In a nutshell, instead of focusing on cutting down your ego, focus on strengthening the relationship with your higher self. Because the truth is, they're two completely different things.

You may be going through a particularly challenging (as well as spiritually and emotionally painful) time right now. Know that you are not alone. More and more people today seem to be experiencing a sense of doom or hopelessness because the world around them has become confusing and disorienting. With increasing tensions from global tragedies, over a decade of war, and divisive elections, poll after poll shows that people are losing faith in many things, from government to religion.

These challenges and crises have the purpose of helping you reconnect to what's real, to your higher self, your higher consciousness—which just so happens to hold the key to their resolution. Crisis serves as a catalyst to discovering your divine purpose—your unique contribution to these end times and the Golden Age that's coming.

I know this because it's what I discovered firsthand. Years ago, in the mid-eighties, a colleague at my first engineering job after college told me that he was intuitive and he knew that at some point in the future, I'd help a lot of people by doing something "new." I began to search for this life purpose ... for decades. But it wasn't until I experienced a major crisis in my own life (one that led me on a deep search for answers) that I finally began to discover what that higher purpose was. Crisis is the driving force for creativity, growth and evolution.

Your crisis will catalyze your spiritual reconnecting and awakening process. Although the reconnecting process works at any time, you are much more likely to seek a deeper connection (and make changes in your life direction) when your life is not working to your satisfaction. So, you might want to view your challenges and crises as catalysts for reconnecting, as the higher self's way of making sure you reconnect, and, through the reconnecting and awakening process, a way to discover your higher purpose and contribute your inner gifts and creativity.

Your higher self is the source of your creativity and potential, your unique inner brilliance. The more you align with your higher consciousness, the less painful your life will be, the more you'll transform yourself and understand the bigger picture to your life, and the more joyful your life will become. Your higher self will give you a new *perspective*.

So how do you align with your higher self and activate the awakening process? There are five simple steps to the spiritual awakening process.

Step 1. Learn to recognize your higher self through meditation, inner examination and "checking in" with yourself.

The first step in the process is to become aware of your higher self, to learn to recognize your higher self's guidance (so that you can distinguish your inner guidance from societal conditionings and outer expectations), and to ask your higher self to help you reconnect.

Are you ready to begin the process? As I said before, your higher self knows you better than you know yourself. Your higher self knows what you respond to, but you must be willing to reconnect to it with your conscious mind, intentions and actions. Although your higher self is your gateway to the divine plan and the divine plan is assured, the process of reconnecting to your higher self is not automatic, and no one can do it for you. It will take conscious effort on your part. You must be willing to take the first steps. Indicating to yourself that you are willing and ready will help activate the process.

The best way to show that you're ready to begin the process is to meditate and pay attention to your "sacred space." Your sacred space is your center, the area defined by the heart, the "soul seed," and the solar plexus. The heart is located slightly left of your chest area, behind the rib cage. The soul seed is located at the center of the breastbone where your ribs meet, and the solar plexus is below the sternum about an inch or two above the navel. You don't have to pinpoint where your sacred space is exactly, only to have an idea of its general location. Then you will do two things: you will meditate with your attention on this area, and you will "check in" to this area several times a day.

Remember that your goal is to develop a stronger, deeper, clearer relationship with your higher self, which may require a meditation that's different than what you're used to. Instead of using a guided meditation to visualize pictures or "what you want," the purpose of this meditation is to calm and center yourself, to try to "feel into" or focus on your sacred space.

The Heart & Soul Meditation: The Counsel of Light recommended a special meditation for connecting within called the "heart and soul" meditation—which you would practice twice daily. (While you may use whatever meditation you like while focusing on your sacred space, the following meditation works really well for connecting to your heart and soul.)

Meditate by placing your left hand on your heart and your right hand over your soul seed—which will help you focus on this area. Then imagine a circle going clockwise around your left hand and a circle going counterclockwise around your right hand, the two imaginary circles connecting together to form a figure eight lying on its side—the symbol for infinity. Putting your hands on your sacred space has the added benefit of calming the body, so you relax and achieve a deeper state of meditation.

The Counsel of Light said, "It's very simple: You take your hands, you put them on your body, you start the wave going, and you stay with that as long as you can and the more you do it, the less afraid you'll be, the more wisdom you'll have, and the more you'll understand ..."

The "wave" mentioned above is the infinity symbol you're tracing around your hands as you're meditating. This meditation connects your heart (which symbolizes your present life) with your higher self (which symbolizes your infinite life) right under your hands.

Try to meditate for about 10 to 15 minutes in the morning when you awaken, and then 10 to 15 minutes at night (or as long as you can before you fall asleep). I like to meditate lying down in bed at night, and again when I wake up in the morning. When you have more time, meditate longer. And if you find yourself not having even five or ten minutes to meditate one morning, you can meditate by imagining your hands on your heart and soul doing the wave while you're washing the dishes or feeding the baby or walking from the parking lot to your place of business.

For me, 10-15 minutes in the morning and at night was enough for the process to begin working. Also, meditating before I fell asleep helped me to fall asleep, and to sleep better when my life was stressful. Plus, later on in the process I began to awaken from my sleep knowing that I (my consciousness) had been in a place I called "the void." The void was very peaceful and calming even when my outer life was not.

Meditation is an ideal time to reconfirm your commitment to your higher self and to ask any questions you may have, but don't rush with the questions at first. Try to get calm and connect within first. (You might feel a slight tingling sensation in that area, even the first time you meditate this way.)

Father Moore said that meditation should be described as "how to listen to God." He said that the answers to any questions you may have will be whispered in your heart. And he shared with us Pokahontas' prayer for help: "Listen, Listen God please listen, until I hear you hearing me. For I know when I hear you hearing, I know I shall be well."

After you become familiar with the heart and soul meditation and can do it almost automatically, you'll want to "listen" by placing your attention on any feelings that come into your awareness. You may notice a subtle feeling such as an inner warmth or energy in your center near your heart. If you feel an inner warmth, a "buzz," a fluttering, or you have a feeling of "spiraling upwards," you were able to "get the wave going" and connect with your higher self. (This is how my higher self helped me to recognize my higher self when all this was new to me.)

After a while, the warm feelings will come with a message from your higher self. This guidance may come at any time, even when you're not meditating. You could be driving down the street, for example, and all of the sudden you start feeling this exquisite energy in the center of your body. Moments later, you get an idea or an insight. In fact, I got used to anticipating and then receiving messages from my higher self (in the form of words or ideas that popped into my head) whenever I felt that nice warmth in the center of my chest.

In order to have complete trust in your higher self, you will need to become confident with distinguishing your inner guidance from your mental conditionings and outer expectations. Much of the time this should be easy, although you may need to do some inner examination. For example, you may ask yourself, "Where did that idea (or belief or desire or value) come from? Was it conditioned into me by society, or is it really me? Is it really my truth, or has it been handed down to me by the establishment? When it's difficult to distinguish between what's really you and what you were conditioned to believe, the feelings from your sacred space will help you to discern the difference.

Because of my strong intention to be guided by my higher self, I began the heart and soul meditation in the spring of 2002 and practiced it religiously, even as I received flashes of insight that my higher self was somehow involved in creating the very predicament from which I wished to be freed.

And now that I think about it, the Counsel of Light never took me through a guided meditation where I had to visualize myself in some peaceful, beautiful environment. My goal was to reconnect as directly and as quickly as possible in order to receive divine guidance for my life. Looking back now, I realize that I received a very effective way to reconnect to my higher self. Indeed, the Counsel of Light called this meditation a "shot in the arm" for connecting with the divine. When you're ready to commit to the process, the heart and soul meditation will work beautifully for you, too.

Checking in: Besides the meditation, I began a practice that I called "checking in." Several times a day, I "checked in" to my sacred space and noticed how it felt. I figured that preparing myself for receiving insights and guidance from my higher self by anticipating the guidance would help "kick start" the process, as well as help me notice the guidance when it came.

Several times a day, place your attention on your sacred space and notice how you feel. It just takes 30 seconds to a minute of your time. You can do this in front of the computer, in the office, or during a bathroom break. Is there a feeling, a thought or a message from your higher consciousness that you ought to take note of? When you "check in" several times a day you're preparing yourself to receive messages from your higher self by consciously anticipating them rather than ignoring them or letting them go by unnoticed (and later regretting that you did).

I'm sure you can recall a time when you had a hunch about something, ignored it, and later wished you didn't. We all need to break the habit of ignoring our intuition and deepest feelings and this practice is an effective way to do this. Checking in helps to awaken an ability in you that's innate, but temporarily dormant. It helps you awaken to your inner power—the power of a shaman.

Paying attention to your sacred space and the thoughts and feelings that seem to arise from it (usually uplifting and empowering) will also help you recognize and discern your inner guidance from the thoughts, feelings and beliefs that come from outer influences and mental conditionings.

Are you open to receive guidance from your higher self? Is your heart open to receive guidance regarding your divine purpose? This is, by the way, what it means to be "open to receive." You're open to receive "energy" from the universe, that comes through your higher self.

Step 2. Follow through on your inner guidance.

Once you master the heart and soul meditation and spend some time learning to recognize the feelings and thoughts that come from your higher self, the next logical step in the process is to follow through with the guidance you receive as promptly and as consistently as possible. Remember that first will come the warm, uplifting feelings, and then the thoughts ... and then it's time to follow through.

Make the commitment and build up the courage to follow through on your inner guidance promptly and consistently. If you consider yourself a beginner, your higher self will most likely have you begin with little things that will help build your trust. For example, you may receive guidance (in the form of a feeling or a thought) to call an old friend or a family member, to write down an insight, or to do something in a particular order that isn't your normal way of doing things. Go ahead and follow through with your inner guidance as soon as you possibly can and notice what happens as a result.

When something favorable happens as a result of following through, your trust in your intuition and in your connection with your higher self will grow. And when you're confident enough to follow through with your intuition in a timely and consistent manner, you'll place yourself in the favorable events, synchronicities, and experiences of flow that will continue to build your trust.

As you continue to learn to listen to and respond to your higher self, your confidence and trust will continue to grow until you begin to *trust your inner self more than anything or anyone outside of yourself*, even in the face of contradictory advice from someone whom you consider to be an expert in his or her field. This is your goal. (They may be the expert, but they do not know you or your situation as well as you know yourself. And certainly, they don't know your higher life plan.)

To be clear, you can and should learn from experts, you can and should weigh the pros and cons before you take certain actions. But ultimately, after you've informed yourself and asked for higher guidance, you go with your intuition.

Your goal is to have the relationship with your higher self be *at least as* real and as important to you as any of your other relationships. Think about this for a moment. How can you be happy if you continue to ignore your heart? (This, by the way, is my understanding of Wynn Free's channeled instructions to, "Open your heart chakra slightly more than half.")

I emphasize the words "at least as" in the previous paragraph because they hold the key to activating the magic of Interconnectedness and synchronicity in your life. I feel this is an important milestone, as things will get really interesting in your life from this point on. It's when you're beginning to follow through with your divine purpose (your contribution in the divine plan) and the "universe" rewards you (promptly and consistently, too) with new insights and favorable synchronicities that will help you fulfill that higher purpose. I call this important milestone "critical mass." Some people refer to it as the "Law of Attraction," or "being in alignment."

In the New Age community, I noticed that "critical mass" referred to the percentage of the population needed in order to make a significant shift or leap in humanity's consciousness. However, I found critical mass to be much more useful in the context of one's individual life (the place where all transformation originates). When you reach critical mass, you begin to tap into the power of a shaman and receive the gifts of Interconnectedness—favorable synchronicities, amazing insights, signs from the universe, flow, universal cooperation, and more—and these gifts begin to show up for you promptly and consistently, too. Rather than happening occasionally, they happen daily. Rather than being the exception, it becomes a way of life.

When you get on your true path and follow through despite the obstacles, you will receive assistance and feedback from the universe. The reason for this is your higher self has a strong "vested interest" in helping you fulfill your higher purpose. And you'll also notice that when you follow through on your inner guidance and happen to benefit in some way, everyone who's involved also benefits. It's a win-win-win situation.

The universe will support you by bringing you—sometimes on a "just in time" basis—exactly what you need to fulfill your higher purpose. You just need to get to a point where you're "aligned" and you trust enough in your higher self, in the divine plan, to go through with your inner guidance.

The following is an excerpt from the entity Abraham, channeled by Esther Hicks, that I received in an email several years ago: "It is Abraham's desire to help you remember the art of alignment first—then action. Alignment first—then conversation. Alignment first—then interaction. Alignment first—then anything else. Your relationships will all fall easily into alignment once you tend to this fundamental primary relationship first."

When you cultivate this fundamental primary relationship first (when the relationship with your higher self is at least as real and as important to you as any of your other relationships), not only will your relationships fall into place, everything else in your life will, too, including your life purpose and ultimate success. This is because everything and everyone is connected to you through the Interconnectedness and your higher self is the gateway to Interconnectedness. Strengthening your relationship with your higher self is the key to all of it.

The following is an example of what you can expect once you get into the habit of following through with your inner guidance promptly and consistently.

In May of 2009 I visited New York City and was invited by my friend D. to attend a fundraiser party in the Lower East Side. When I called him on his cell phone the evening of the event, the first thing he said was, "Christine, I have to tell you that you have perfect timing. I just stepped into a part of the building that's actually quiet and I can hear you well. If you had called a minute before, we wouldn't have been able to have a conversation."

I told him that having perfect timing was merely a "side effect" of listening to your inner guidance and relayed to him another similar story. About two summers before, a friend F. did a road trip from California to Alaska for several weeks. He stayed mostly at campgrounds and spent some time in the unpopulated areas of Canada. When I got an inner nudge to call him on his cell phone to see how his trip was going, we hadn't been in contact for almost a couple of weeks.

"Did you try calling me before?" F. asked.

"No, this is the first time I tried calling you since you left for your trip," I said.

"Well, that's interesting because this is the first time I'm able to get mobile service in several days. You have good timing." F. happened to be staying at a campsite in Northern Canada that actually had reception.

I have experienced—too many times to remember—people telling me, "I was just thinking of calling you" when I called them. But it's these quirky stories like the examples above that I remember best.

Perhaps you're thinking, "Big deal! What does this have to do with fulfilling your higher purpose?" A great deal, I would think. If you had perfect timing, you'd be in the right place at the right time all the time every time. You can achieve this kind of timing by being "in tune" with yourself and following your inner guidance promptly and consistently.

There's a good reason for this. Your higher self has access to the bigger picture, to things your "ego mind" isn't aware of (yet) and your eyes cannot see at the moment. Your higher self is your direct access to Interconnectedness, to your spirit guides, and to your part in the divine plan. Your higher self (along with the other souls involved) actually planned and mapped out this plan in the "higher realms." That's why I can say that when you consciously reconnect to your higher self and follow through with your inner guidance, you'll fulfill your higher purpose.

When you reconnect to your higher consciousness and develop enough confidence to follow through with your inner guidance promptly and consistently, you'll actually *place yourself* in the favorable events and synchronicities that will help you fulfill your purpose. Furthermore, following through on your inner guidance helps you become aware of gifts and talents you might not be conscious of right now, because they're hidden in your soul. And all of this will help you believe in yourself.

The following story about believing in oneself (one's Self) was inspired by an email I received from Noah St. John, author of *The Book of Afformations,* soon after the death of the musical icon Prince.

Noah wrote that Prince's belief in himself and his vision was so strong that he signed a recording contract at the age of 19. Then he fought for—and got—total creative control over his first three albums. (Which is kind of unheard of in the record industry.) *"I believe in myself and understand my vision better than any of you do. So I'm going to do things the way I want to do them,"* wrote Noah about Prince.

Then Noah asked his community, What about you? Do you believe in yourself? Have you stood up for your vision?

This inspired me to write a blog post about how following my intuition helped me stand up for my vision, and how you can harness the power of Prince for your vision, too. (I.e. The power of a shaman: Prince was a musical genius and shaman in his own way.)

Late in 2006, I hired a top-notch editor in the spiritual niche to edit my first book. Although she was tops in her field and I was open to her input, I knew my book needed a "light" editing—language, grammar and verb tense—rather than content editing. I was confident my book was a memoir of my spiritual reconnecting process and "the Universe" supported its writing. What I mean is that amazing, favorable synchronicities happened almost daily that became content for my book, once I tapped into the reconnecting / creative process. It's how my book got written.

My editor recommended I write a "how-to" book instead, rather than a memoir of my process. After all, she explained, you're an unknown.

We exchanged a few emails and I thought I finally convinced her that I needed to do it my way. This was a book on intuition; it made sense to honor my higher self's guidance, I had explained. She finally agreed.

But then, rather than honoring her word, she spent many hours rewriting it. She deleted many wonderful, true-life stories and repeated the same bland, Buddhist-inspired message over and over again that I wasn't even in agreement with—exactly what I asked her *not* to do. Then she sent me a big fat invoice.

Because she hadn't honored our agreement, I could use maybe half of her work. I sent her a letter explaining the issues, including references to our previous emails, and paid her slightly more than half of the invoice. I felt I was generous and fair.

But she wanted every penny. Two months later, I got a letter from a collection agency. I wrote the agency a letter explaining that my editor hadn't followed standard industry practices. Then she wrote the agency, stating that in her 38 years of service, nobody had ever taken issue with any of her invoices, or advice. I wrote another letter in rebuttal, thinking that would be the end of it.

But it wasn't. About a month later, around June 2007, I received a letter from a law firm in San Francisco. Too upset to look inside, I shoved the letter unopened between the seats of my car.

A few days later, while doing the final polishing of my manuscript and listening to music online, I got an intuitive message to go get the dreaded letter from my car. (I usually don't listen to the radio while writing because it's distracting, but I was inspired to do so that day. Well, I was just following my intuition ...)

The letter stated that if the balance of the editor's bill wasn't paid immediately, a lawsuit would be filed against me. Furthermore, additional amounts would be owed in the event of litigation.

I trudged back into my house upset and disheartened, heading toward my bedroom, back to my computer, my spirits crushed. Nobody believed in me. And not only did my editor not believe in me, she was now planning on suing me.

But as I walked into my bedroom I heard the following words being sung: "She a-howlin' about the front rent, she'll be lucky to get any back rent, she ain't gonna get none of it!" It was George Thorogood, singing with his "Bad to the Bone" attitude.

This was a sign from the Universe! I knew it because these kinds of crazy things happened to me almost daily, sometimes several times a day, when I was writing my book! Inspired, I wrote a final letter to the law office explaining *exactly* why I wouldn't be paying the balance. And I haven't heard from the lawyers or the editor ever since.

I self-published my book so I could have it the way I wanted it, the way the Universe was showing me to do it. A few years later, it was recognized by traditional publisher North Atlantic Books as one of four "notable spiritual awakening memoirs" of the last several years, along with *Eat Pray Love*, *The Happiness Project*, and *Star Sister*.

By the way, this book that you hold in your hand, originally published November 2009 and sold from my website (later updated and made available on Amazon) *is* my "how-to" book. So you see, I took that editor's advice after all.

Now what about you? When you reconnect with your higher self and follow through with your inner guidance, you'll tap into the power of a shaman, a shaman who has dream visions, and the Universe will support you. And that's because the Universe supports *the dreams that arise from your soul.*

While not every little development will be extremely important to your life purpose, you have to admit that favorable synchronicities such as the ones I shared so far will help you become confident in your connection to your higher self, in your ability to "read" your inner guidance, in yourself, and in the divine plan.

The further along I was in the process outlined in this chapter, the more whatever I needed to fulfill my higher purpose (part of which is the writing of this book) simply "showed up" when I needed it, often within 24 hours of thinking about what it was that I needed. Sometimes a new insight would come to me in the middle of the night, sometimes what I needed came in the mail, or in an email, or in a conversation I had that day. I suppose this is the "Law of Attraction" at work. The Law of Attraction helps you fulfill your *higher purpose* (as opposed to the simplistic message promoted by some Law of Attraction experts that you can use it to get "what you want" from the Universe, like a bright red sports car or a brand-new bike).

When you get on the path of your higher purpose, the Law of Attraction will work for you, too. The catch is, you won't know what your *divine* purpose is until you've been following your inner guidance for a while, and then there may still be some surprises. This is why visualizing "what you want" (i.e. what that ego consciousness part of you happens to want at that moment) has not been working for most people.

There's no need to worry that you won't achieve your desires; you will. You'll achieve your deepest desires and much more when you follow the path of your divine purpose. As a materials engineer with a master's in environmental and energy studies I certainly did not visualize that I'd write books on spiritual awakening and planetary transformation—but that's where my circumstances and higher purpose led me.

Your higher purpose will reflect not only your current talents and ambitions but the hidden gifts and talents of that God-spark within you that's been around forever and has experienced many lifetimes. Makes sense, doesn't it? What your limitedly-aware mind may want in the moment and what your higher self has planned for you may seem different, but after you get on the path of your divine purpose you'll understand and will be pleasantly surprised.

However, just because I say that whatever you need to fulfill your life purpose will show up doesn't mean you should wait for everything to just come to you—it means you do the things you can do in the moment and the universe will assist you with the things that aren't yet clear or resolved or complete for you.

An example: When I was thinking about what I'd need to learn so I could create an ebook and sell it online, I received an email with an offer of a report that would teach me about the writing, marketing and selling of ebooks. The timing was perfect and the price reasonable. Then my marketing mentor happened to create a free teleseminar on ebooks for her monthly subscribers. Assistance from the universe takes on many forms and also helps confirm that you're on the right track.

Step 3. Ask for clear guidance when you need it, and pay attention to "signs from the universe."

When you have mastered the heart and soul meditation and have begun to follow through with your inner guidance, you'll likely encounter a situation where you feel like you're stuck in a quagmire and don't know what to do, or are afraid of making the wrong move. You may desire divine guidance, but you just don't trust yourself enough yet to interpret your thoughts and feelings correctly because you're stressed or afraid. When you're under stress, it seems harder to connect to your higher self and have confidence in that connection, or in the divine plan. This is a good time to ask your higher self for guidance so clear it cannot be easily misinterpreted. (Remember, your higher self knows you better than you know yourself.)

I have received what I called "signs from the universe" on a number of occasions and the signs came quickly after I asked for them, too. (At that point in my process, I was already gaining trust in my higher self and was pretty confident I'd go through with the guidance, once it was clear to me.)

The following is an example taken from my first book.

Early along in my reconnecting process (in 2003) I had to make a decision about moving forward with my life purpose and moving into a new home, or staying stuck. It was a difficult decision. I found a small rental nearby, and the landlady and I got along.

However, something didn't feel right about it—which I blamed on the stress of my decision to move. When the time came to give the potential landlady my decision, I couldn't do it. I was too stressed out.

I sought advice from a friend who told me to try to calm myself and listen to my guidance. Then I got the idea to say a short prayer and ask for guidance so clear that it could not be misinterpreted. I lay down on my bed, trying to relax, trying to be quiet and calm so I could hear / receive the clear guidance. But it didn't come.

An hour or so later I got up to pick up my kids from school. I got into my car, remaining quiet, still waiting for that clear guidance from the universe. Then a half block from the school my right hand turned the radio on to blasting. In that moment, Bono of the rock band U2 sang the following words: "I still haven't found what I'm looking for." This was my clear sign!

The same thing happened again a month later when I had to make a decision about the next rental I was considering, only this time I turned the radio on as soon as I left my driveway. Bono sang those same words again.

The "universe" finally let me know when the timing was right for moving by providing me with some crazy amazing synchronicities. (For example, the new landlady happened to email me at the same moment I was reading her rental ad on Craigslist.)

When you look back though, you'll find that the signs were there all along (for example, a feeling that "something's not right here"); it's just that you weren't quite ready to trust yourself yet.

Besides asking for clear guidance, you can also begin your day by asking your higher self, "What's the best thing I can do today to move my project forward?" Or you can say, "Help me fulfill my life purpose. Send me what I need to do my work for today." Or before you go to sleep at night, you can take note of the day's challenges and ask for guidance and assistance while you sleep so that you awaken with some helpful insights.

Feel free to use your own words. There's no magic in these specific words. Rather, the magic lies in your relationship with your higher self and in your connection to divine plan.

Besides receiving clear answers when you ask for divine guidance, sometimes you'll receive what I refer to as a "sign from the universe" two or even three times in a short period of time—even when you didn't ask for it. It's a good idea to pay attention to such signs. It may be the "universe" trying to tell you something. Or it may be your higher self trying to get your attention, or your higher self teaching you something. The following is an excellent example.

A friend F. was planning an annual camping trip for the end of the summer (it was 2009) but didn't know where he wanted to go. F. had already been to Alaska and the East Coast and back and had enjoyed it a great deal. He asked for my advice.

I suggested he visit the Banff area in Alberta, Canada. I said this because the week before, I had received two emails that referred to Banff. One was from someone from my own list who asked a question about ley lines and the activation of electromagnetic energies in areas such as Lake Louise and Banff. This person wanted to know whether it would be beneficial to visit these natural areas to achieve the most personal growth. The other email mentioned the exquisite energies and amazing beauty of Banff. This was odd, as normally I don't get any emails about Banff.

Banff would be the perfect choice for F., I thought. Besides, F. was as an electrical engineer who used to work with magnetic tapes. He could go investigate those electromagnetic energies. (Yes, I wanted to send F. on a mission to look into these "energy matters" because I couldn't do it myself—at least not that year.)

I shared my idea with F., but I don't think he was too thrilled about it. He said he was leaning towards the Oregon and Washington coasts.

A few days before leaving on his trip, F. and I met for a hike and bumped into his neighbor who was a regular on the trail. She wore a t-shirt from Banff, which I complimented her on. Then as she walked away I said to F., "Did you see that? Her t-shirt read Banff. The universe is telling you to go to Banff."

But his mind was set. (I suppose despite numerous conversations about Interconnectedness, divine plan, intuition and signs from the universe, he still liked to think that he was doing his own thing.) He left for Oregon the Wednesday before Labor Day.

On Labor Day I received a call from F., telling me that he was in Banff! He explained that it was raining the whole time on the coast so he just kept driving ... until he got to Banff, where it was bright and sunny and everything was just right. "So what is it you wanted me to look at?" he asked.

I suppose this also answers the question of whether or not visiting exquisite areas such as Lake Louise and Banff is beneficial for your personal growth—well, especially if you are guided to visit those areas by receiving two or more interesting signs from the universe in a short period of time.

Step 4. Prepare to change your mindset.

Prepare to let go of old, false beliefs and mental conditionings. (Remember to examine where the belief or idea came from. Is it really you?) Old beliefs and mental conditionings (about yourself, about others, and about the world) get in the way of your progress and will need to be adjusted or released.

It's probably best to start with the beliefs you have about yourself and what you think you're capable of. That's what this spiritual awakening process is about, anyway. However, you won't need to contemplate or agonize over exactly what those beliefs are and you won't need to make long lists of beliefs you want to change—unless you want to, of course. You'll find they'll come up for you organically, without much conscious effort.

The good news is, as you get further along in the process, your new firsthand experiences will help override any false or negative beliefs and mental conditionings you have about yourself almost automatically. It's okay to keep your current understanding until you find a greater truth to replace it with. Know that the greater trust in your inner guidance and in yourself, the newfound insights and the wisdom you receive, and your new habits, capacities, and confidence will help you change your mindset.

The following is an example of how I dealt with "negative thoughts and beliefs" that were more than just thoughts—they were my reality. This example will help you when your beliefs are so entrenched they don't occur to you as beliefs but as reality, as "the way things are."

In 2002 I began to think about writing a book about "explaining love;" because the Counsel of Light had suggested this. The problem was, I was not a trained writer nor expert on love. I was an introverted, left-brained engineer who knew her writing was mediocre at best.

I wasn't even aware of what I was supposed to write about. The pessimistic thoughts in my head, "Your writing sucks" and, "You've got nothing to say and you know it" were not just thoughts—they were my reality. I had every reason to take them seriously. Four years later in 2006 (after some major events in my life), I showed my third draft to a top-rate editor. "Write a how-to book instead," she recommended. (How-to books are much easier to write than memoirs.) Negative thoughts confirmed by an expert!

I was distressed and annoyed, yet I knew I had no choice but to keep going on the path of following my inner guidance. Even though she was the expert, following my inner guidance had gotten me that far and the daily support I received from the universe validated this path. Furthermore, I felt it was my story that would give me credibility, the interesting things that happened once I began to follow my intuition; my educational background certainly gave me zero credibility for writing a how-to book on spirituality. (I also had good, logical reasons why continuing on my path made sense.) I explained to my editor that since this was going to be a book on intuition I needed to follow my intuition—but that idea didn't go over well.

So I focused daily on developing my writing capacity. (My inner guidance helped me with doing this as quickly as possible.) My negative thoughts motivated me to do my best, and I went over my draft at least three more times. And as my writing improved, those negative thoughts finally lessened. (One could say that my daily focus on my writing helped cure my negative thoughts about my writing.)

In the end, my book turned out to be a finalist in the autobiography / memoir category for the 2008 National Best Books Awards, and North Atlantic Books recognized it as one of four "notable spiritual awakening memoirs" of the last several years.

If I had simply ignored my negative thoughts (or just replaced them with positive ones) I wouldn't have worked as diligently and I wouldn't have made as much progress. And I can actually say that I'm grateful for those negative thoughts.

Connecting to your higher consciousness and letting go of outdated beliefs and conditionings go hand in hand. Also, when you let go of cherished beliefs you suspect may be false (your suspicion may be your higher self whispering to you), you enable insights and new possibilities to come through that previously were blocked by those beliefs. Letting go unblocks the flow of creativity and abundance in your life and helps you "spiral upward," which makes it easier to achieve your heart's desires in the end.

Step 5. Continue the process to discover and fulfill your divine purpose—your unique contribution to the "New Earth."

Continue the process to find your higher purpose—your unique and brilliant contribution to the "New Earth." The process described above will not only reconnect you to your higher self for guidance, it will be what you need to discover your higher purpose—your soul's blueprint for success. Your higher purpose will be your entry key, your initiation into, and your contribution to the New Earth / Golden Age.

You may need to recommit to your higher self again and again. You'll find that you will be tested; you'll come across an obstacle and will need to make a choice about how to continue. Will you recommit to your divine purpose no matter what it takes? It's much easier to keep on the path when you can see the bigger picture.

I found that I had breakthroughs in creativity, productivity, insights, connection, etc. almost immediately after I changed my mindset and recommitted to my higher self and purpose. These breakthroughs, and the corresponding feelings of accomplishment engendered in me, increased my trust in myself and in my connection to divine plan and motivated me to keep going … to complete my two books, for example.

Once you feel comfortable with the process and have experienced some results that helped you gain some confidence in your connection, it's a good time to include another meditation in your daily regimen. This meditation is called the "Heaven and Earth" meditation, and it will help you with increasing the flow of energy (i.e. consciousness, or healing energy) between the dimensions (which will further help to integrate the dimensions). It's a slight modification of a meditation I learned in a Soul Recognition workshop given by Flo Aeveia Magdalena of Soul Support Systems.

Heaven and Earth Meditation: Standing with your feet about shoulder length apart, your hands hanging loosely at your sides, knees slightly bent, eyes closed and exhaling slowly, imagine sunlight or energy from the Sun (or galactic center, or Source, or God, or the dimensions above; just pick one) coming down to the top of your head, entering your body at the crown and going down through your body in a straight line, down your spine all the way through to the bottom of your feet, all the way down through the ground and bedrock, to the center core of the Earth. Then inhaling slowly, imagine this energy reflect back from the very core of the Earth, through the different layers of Earth, back through the bottom of your feet all the way through your body to the top of your head, then back up to the Sun or the higher dimensions. Imagine also that this light energy is as coherent as a laser beam.

Repeat this exercise several times, imagining the energy or light flowing up and then down; inhale energy going up, exhale energy going down, with a short pause at each end point. Try to do this meditation at least once a day, twice is preferred, for about three to ten minutes each. Alternatively, for some variety you can imagine this energy going out to the cosmos with each out-breath and coming back into your inner core with each in-breath.

This is a simple practice you can do anywhere (although whenever possible, it's a good idea to do this meditation outdoors standing with your bare feet on the Earth).

When you do this meditation, you can expect the connection to both your physical environment (your normal level awareness) and to the heavenly or angelic realms (the guidance from your higher self, your guides, your dreams) to strengthen and integrate and the energy (consciousness) to flow in between with more clarity and ease. I call this process becoming a "superconductor of creative energy."

I was inspired to recommit to doing the Heaven & Earth meditation after a dream I had while writing my first book (the memoir). The following describes my dream.

With a pounce onto my chest, our kitten awakened me from a dream the day I would revise the chapter titled, Superconductor. In the dream, I was on my way to Alaska as a passenger in what looked like a new, comfortable European-style city bus. I was aware that I've never been to Alaska before, only to Canada, and I was thinking that going to Alaska would be as easy as going to Canada.

The bus traveled through a picturesque, green valley in between beautiful snow-capped peaks, maybe ten miles from one side to the other. The scenery reminded me of the Davos, Switzerland area, still snowy in the higher elevations though it was almost summer. The bus meandered, switchbacking up an incline, went here and there, stopping for passengers to get on, taking its time. Impatient, I asked a woman sitting next to me how long this trip to Alaska was supposed to take.

"It'll be around four hours," she said.

Four hours? That was way too long for me! I wanted to get there sooner! I explained to her that if I drove my own car, it would take me only two hours. So I decided to get off public transportation and drive my own vehicle. I pulled the signal to stop and got off the bus. That's when the cat woke me up.

Was this dream telling me to avoid mass transportation and public direction and follow my own, to power up my "vehicle" and drive up the spiral of evolution? Most definitely.

Furthermore, I got another valuable insight from that dream: Alaska doesn't have to be viewed as some destination or end point because in reality, once you get to Alaska, there's a whole new, big wonderful state to explore!

By the way, that's the dream that inspired me to recommit to the Heaven and Earth meditation, to speed up the creative process.

Your breakthroughs in creativity, wisdom and insights are the hidden gifts that are part of your "inner repertoire." Remember that your higher self is your direct access to the wisdom of your infinite life, your connection to the larger universe, and the gateway to the abundance and the unexpected blessings of the universe (or, if you prefer, God). In other words, when you reconnect to your higher self and gain enough confidence to follow through on your inner guidance consistently, you activate your "super-conscious" mind.

It's a good idea to write your insights into a journal that you keep near your bed. This doesn't mean you have to spend years writing a memoir and publishing it like I did, although who knows? ... it might. However, it's a good idea to keep track of your new ideas and insights. Your new insights will help transform your life and help you fulfill your higher purpose.

Continue this process and you'll eventually be able to make complete sense of your life, which will give you not only true self-confidence but also the inner peace your heart longs for. Although some may believe that when you follow your intuition you might as well throw logic and reasoning out the window, this is not true at all. It only appears that way from our limited point of view, from our limited understanding. (Remember that your higher self is in touch with the larger plan—which your mind cannot currently grasp and your eyes cannot see at the moment.)

In fact, the new paradigm, higher-level understanding attained through the process of reconnecting with your higher self will make *more* logical sense (as it should). Also, when you begin to understand the bigger picture of your life, your intuition and your logical reasoning will begin to go hand in hand and you will no longer feel that you are fighting the inner battle between your mind and your heart. And when you stop the inner battle, the outer battles will also stop.

Meditation alone is never enough. Learning to trust your higher consciousness and following through so that it gets integrated into your life is what it takes for you to become "One" within. Many spiritual teachers talk about a concept called "Oneness;" which you will attain when you integrate with your higher self / higher consciousness. Oneness within will then create outer Oneness, and Oneness in the world.

Ultimately, you'll come to understand your life story from the higher-level perspective of your soul and this higher-level understanding is what will set you free. You will know who you are, why you are here, and whether you have fulfilled your original goals. And when you set yourself free, you'll set everyone else in your life free, including even your worst enemy.

Once this happens, consider yourself spiritually awakened, "ascended in consciousness," or enlightened. In other words, a shaman.

What I Learned and What's Important to Know

The world is changing on many levels at the moment and many of us are concerned about our family's security and safety, as well as our own. No matter what you're going through right now, know that you're at the perfect place in your higher life plan and that the outcome is assured. Know that you are not alone and that many are going through similar experiences. Know also that there has never been a greater opportunity in the entirety of human history (and in the entirety of your personal history) for positive change to occur than right now.

If you knew that everything and everyone was part of divine plan and that everyone, regardless of who they were or what they were doing at the moment, was playing into divine plan (even though they considered themselves to be acting independently, or above the law, or appeared to be acting out of arrogance), there'd be no need to be afraid, would there?

When you go through the process of reconnecting within and gaining trust in your higher self and in your connection and understanding of divine plan, you'll naturally learn to be less and less afraid. By following the steps outlined in the previous chapter, you'll gain the wisdom and understanding to see yourself through whatever situation you happen to be at the moment. You'll be more proactive and you'll realize that the process is working; you are reconnecting to your wisdom and are beginning to understand your life from a deeper level perspective. You'll gain some real perspective. Plus, you'll see through any nonsense that comes your way trying to distract you. You'll begin to see that the future does look promising. And in fact, you'll begin to feel uplifted and exhilarated when before, you were used to feeling hopeless and afraid.

In this chapter, I hope to boost your courage and resolve and give you a "shot in the arm" that will help lessen any remaining fear regarding the shift in consciousness and the changes happening on the planet and in your life. You'll still need to gain trust in your higher self (and in the divine plan) and all that is up to you, but when you understand the bigger picture you'll release your fear much faster.

It's okay to feel *some* fear. Fear is a good thing when it drives you to connect deeper and to take effective action. You can be afraid and still have faith in your higher life plan. You can follow your inner guidance feeling some fear. You can be afraid and still keep going. Fear can help you strive to be and do your best. Fear can be your friend.

An example: I had some fear when writing the original version of this book back in the summer of 2009. It was my first ebook. I wanted it completed within three months, both the research and the writing, before the Hollywood movie *2012* came out that November. I wanted it to be clear and understandable to the average person—even though I had no idea what, if anything, I was going to discover and there were things I learned during my research that I previously wasn't aware of, such as certain details about the Mayan connection and the astronomy of the 2012 alignments.

The fear I felt in the back of my mind (about not being able to do this well enough in a short period of time) motivated me to focus on this project consistently so that my desired outcome would come to fruition. I focused on achieving the desired outcome by following my intuition and putting in several hours of work on this project daily.

As you may be aware, leaders in the spiritual and New Age movements have been teaching the importance of "focusing on the Light" and using your thoughts, feelings and actions to "attract" what you want to experience in your life and in the world. Focusing on your fears and the things you don't want attracts more of the same, you've been told. If you can learn how to "shift your field of energy," you can begin to shift what shows up in your life from negative to positive. These ideas are the basic concepts of the Law of Attraction.

Yet if the Law of Attraction hasn't been working for you it isn't because you've been doing something wrong, it isn't that you're not good enough, it's not because you have too many "negative thoughts" or can't seem to gain control of your thoughts and feelings, it's not because you haven't forgiven yourself or others, it's not because you aren't "focusing" on the positive or feeling grateful enough, it isn't because you haven't tallied up enough "I AM" affirmations yet or participated in enough rituals, and it's not because you don't deserve your heart's desire. (So get all that garbage out of your head!) It's just that your higher self has a plan for your life that happens to be grander than your limited human consciousness is able to see right this minute.

Your higher self (also referred to as your inner core, your essence, your soul, your connection to God, the true Holy Spirit, your superconsciousness, your inner being, your authentic self, your true self, your subconscious...) has a plan for your life that's greater, nobler, more courageous, more adventurous, more impressive, and bigger-hearted than your human personality self is able to conceive right now. And even though your life path may have taken numerous curious or bizarre detours, ultimately your higher life plan is more perfect than your limited human mind is capable of conceiving at the moment.

There's been a lot of confusion regarding the Law of Attraction the last several years. People have tried to elucidate and elaborate on the Law of Attraction, often using confusing language and vague concepts. Some have gotten close, but I've found that close isn't good enough. Even though the ideas may be close, it's not enough to be close. You need to be precise for things to work. And now you know that the missing ingredient in the Law of Attraction has to do with you fulfilling your higher purpose—your part of the divine plan that will help create a new experience of Light on planet Earth. And now you understand why for most people, "The Law" hasn't worked all that well.

The author Wynn Free made the distinction between individuals oriented toward "service to self" versus "service to others." Those who will "graduate" from this realm will be oriented toward "service to others," according to his channeled sources.

According to what I discovered, when you follow through with your inner guidance and fulfill your divine purpose, not only will you benefit, but everyone and everything else will, too. (This is because, as I've already mentioned, your higher self is how you're connected to Interconnectedness—to everyone and everything—and to the divine plan.) By following through on your higher self's guidance and integrating that higher consciousness within you, you are aligning with "service to all" (which happens to include yourself). "Graduation from this realm" refers to this "ascension in consciousness."

Well, it seems that service-to-self isn't working all that well anyway. We are—as the astronomy explains—reorienting toward galactic light, to "service to all." Of course, not everyone will reorient at the same exact time. That would be strange, and it's not part of divine plan. There will be no messiahs showing up that will whisk believers away, or any ET motherships, either. Because there are still lessons that need to be learned don't expect everyone to reorient all at once. Rather, the reorientation will happen in "waves."

For a method to be powerful, you need to learn its distinctions and subtleties. Just touching on it on a surface level isn't enough, just as the instructions to "shift your energy," "follow your intuition" or "orient yourself toward service to others" usually isn't enough. (At least not until you become literate in the area.) Because when you actually do follow your inner guidance promptly and consistently and keep track of what happens as a result there's so much more that you'll begin to understand.

After I wrote my first book (that dreaded memoir that some people have had a hard time with reading) I began to write a series of articles about a larger perspective and understanding that was emerging within me, a perspective that was outside of the drama and the struggle of the human story. I began to project this understanding onto humanity's story, and this helped me view history differently.

A deeper perspective is emerging on the planet, which, if added to our current understanding (that we're in the midst of an awakening process), will create the impetus necessary for real and positive change to occur. This perspective—the perspective of the higher self, or higher consciousness—is beginning to emerge in the collective consciousness. For example, Robert Schwartz writes about it in his book, *Your Soul's Plan: Discovering the Real Meaning of the Life You Planned Before You Were Born*, which I highly recommend.

Part of what's emerging in the collective consciousness is the understanding that we are more responsible for our lives than we've previously believed. This is not meant to promote guilt, but to help empower you, to empower you to make the changes your higher consciousness is guiding you to make.

If you knew that your higher self had planned your life experiences *so that you would grow*, so that you would come to know yourself as the "one who rose to the challenge," wouldn't much of the fear and inertia that prevents you from getting out of your rut and moving forward in your life be alleviated?

And because your higher self had planned everything in your life, including your biggest challenges, you would know that you had whatever you needed to complete those challenges successfully within you. And not only successfully, but in ways that will be unprecedented in human history. In other words, the keys to fulfilling your heart's desires can be found within, by following the process outlined in the previous chapter.

As you begin to do this for yourself, you'll have glimpses of your soul's original plan. Your life will begin to make more sense to you, and you'll begin to understand how it fits into the larger "Earth Experiment," or "Earth game."

On a collective level, if we knew that each and every one of us had a role in planning this Earth Experiment, and if we remembered why we (humanity) agreed to "play the game" in the first place, we'd view the world's crises as opportunities for growth and expansion rather than dreadful things to be avoided. We'd know that we had the power within to complete this Earth game successfully.

I came to understand that we created this earth game a long, long time ago, and with good intentions, too: so that we would learn and grow and come to more fully and authentically express ourselves. So that we'd become the masters of our lives. So that the level of joy and happiness and the depth of experience would heighten, so that the level of appreciation and compassion and love would skyrocket. This earth game was planned for the learning and growth of all.

If you don't experience any major challenges or adversity in your life, there's a limit to how much you can grow. This is why I feel the "fall in consciousness" was not a bad thing. (And the fall of Atlantis was not a bad thing, either.) In my opinion, it was a planned event—planned by our higher consciousness and part of divine plan—that served a brilliant evolutionary function. The fall in consciousness made possible the next step in our evolutionary and spiritual growth.

And if the fall in consciousness wasn't a bad thing, then we can look at the individuals and institutions that kept our consciousness suppressed as not all that bad, either. It was all planned this way with the permission of our higher selves.

If you object to the idea above, I totally get it. But this divine plan isn't something you'd be conscious about. Remember, if you were conscious of it, it wouldn't work nearly as well. Furthermore, the soul does not care too much about temporary feelings and situations. The soul knows it's infinite. The soul knows that this experience in duality, of learning through contrast and extreme challenges, would be temporary, a mere blink in time compared to infinity. And the soul's primary goal is to grow.

We wanted the spiritual growth, our souls wanted to grow. We also understood that if we didn't experience hardships and challenges firsthand, there was a limit to how far we could evolve. During a crisis, you're much more likely to search for creative and inspiring solutions to your problems. Historically, incredible technological as well as social advances resulted from humanity's painful experiences. From the soul's point of view, the resulting growth and inner transformation make the often relatively short-lived crisis well worth it. You get to discover firsthand who you are and what you're truly capable of. And when the transformation occurs and things begin to turn around for you, to appreciate life like never before.

This can be a hard concept to accept, especially when your life isn't working and you feel stuck, not knowing what to do next or where to go. I absolutely understand; I was there myself. I used to think my higher self must have been crazy to think up my life plan, the way my life was unfolding. And I felt powerless to change things because of how making changes would affect others in my life. *My higher self must have been crazy.* (It was a challenge to think this while at the same time trying to reconnect to it for guidance.)

I had to get past that, to reconcile all that in order to move forward—which took a while. Then as I reconnected to my higher self I began to learn how to play the game and it became eye-opening and exhilarating. But it certainly doesn't feel like a game, not until you learn how to play it.

Anyway, as new souls we yearned to learn and grow, to discover who we really were, and the best and quickest way to attain these noble goals was by living through a variety of experiences, including interpersonal difficulties and many other kinds of hardships. But how were we to create *that* knowing who we were, knowing we were all sparks of the One God? The only way we could have created that kind of experiencing (helping each other learn through pain and suffering) was by creating a fall in our collective consciousness. We knew we had to make ourselves forget who we were and from where we came.

And how would that be possible? By engineering a break in our consciousness. Contrary to what you may have been led to believe, the "separation" from your higher self was something your higher self actually engineered. And how could we make that happen? Well, the fall of an advanced civilization (technologically advanced, not necessarily spiritually) such as Atlantis, and a big flood (or two) happened to be a good start.

After a traumatic event such as the fall of a great civilization into the ocean, a new kind of experiencing on this planet would be made possible. A series of traumatic events would further erase the collective memory and force people to focus on the physical, on their own survival. Over time, people would forget their (galactic?) origins, forget who they were and from where they came (different places in the galaxy?), the level of confusion and fear would increase, making everyone more willing to accept the new beliefs that would be given to them by those in power, beliefs that would promote fear, separation and a lowering of consciousness.

The new beliefs (of an angry God or gods, of humanity's sinning and original sin) would promote further separation and strife between brothers, tribes and countries. If you promised what the people wanted (to survive, to be led out of slavery, to be saved), you would likely rise in power. The more fear that was present, the more people would give up their power to you, and the more you'd rise in power. Spiritual enlightenment was not to come from within but from the special rituals you performed. You could make the people believe in anything (even that objects such as golden calves possessed more power than they). You could make the people do anything you wanted (even offer up their food and livestock for the purpose of appeasing a vengeful God).

We forgot that we were the creators of our own experiences and began to believe that we were mere pawns in a game we didn't understand, that we were created by an angry, jealous God (or gods) and were subject to the laws put down by power-hungry tyrants (who held themselves to be above the law and of special origins). We forgot what it was like prior to the fall. A kind of global amnesia took over.

Jesus Christ possessed secret knowledge that was passed down to him from Atlantean ancestors who had known what was coming and had escaped the fall. Some settled in the area known as Galilee, others left for different parts of the world. This particular information—the Jesus-Atlantis connection—was channeled by Carolyn Evers, but I had been aware that both Jesus Christ and Mary Magdalene had attended "ancient mystery schools." (And just what do you suppose those "ancient mysteries" were about?)

Jesus tried to teach the truth—that the truth and the power and the knowing and the "Kingdom of Heaven" could be found within each person, that we were all One, that we were all brothers and sisters from one Source, that there was a divine plan, but perhaps it was too much for the people to reconcile then, given their reality. He knew it wasn't time yet, that the people weren't ready to accept responsibility for that yet, that the dark ages weren't over yet.

Like the Mayans (and the Magi) he was knowledgeable in the cycles of the cosmos. He knew it would take many more years, another age in the future. Still, he impacted the world greatly by teaching and being an example of True Love. Through his teachings, the people would continue to learn and evolve on many levels. He also knew that 2000 years later he'd return (just like everyone else) and he and those closest to him would help introduce the new understanding that was to become available to the world. Only this time, the female would not have to remain silent for fear of stoning and it would be her turn to do much of the work of "remembering," synthesizing, and disseminating of these ideas—which is only fair. (Remember: Freedom, Equality and Brother / Sisterhood.)

But enough of the theorizing and pontificating. I'm no Bible or history scholar; I'm simply sharing my story and the understanding that began to emerge within me once I went through the process described in the previous chapter and finished my first book. You may wish to look into Father Charlie Moore's book *Synthesis Remembered* for clues to our history, as he *is* a scholar of religion and history.

Anyway, what's important to realize is that we did all this for each other, for each other's learning and growth. We knew that the earth "illusion" we created would be instrumental in helping us evolve as quickly as possible. Although we knew that some of our experiences would be extremely difficult (and some we'd have to make amends for), we also were aware that this was the quickest way to spiritual growth and a temporary sacrifice, a temporary phase in our evolution.

I came to understand that each and every person on this planet had agreed to play the game of duality. If your soul hadn't agreed to play this Earth game, you wouldn't be here on this planet at this time. But this isn't something you'd easily "remember." You don't easily remember your past lives either, and for good reasons, too.

If we had known that we were the creators of this Earth game, if we were conscious of all that, we might not have played this game with such complete conviction and seriousness, which would have derailed the learning experiences our souls really wanted. But our souls are powerful, so powerful that we have created an illusion and then lived it as if it were real in order to accomplish the larger goals. As I said, this Earth experience worked because we were largely unconscious of it. (Well, the paradox is that this Earth experience both *is* and *is not* an illusion. However, that discussion is beyond the scope of this book, and something you'll come to realize after you've played with this process for a while.)

Eventually, when we were in the process of learning our final lessons, we'd "remember" that this Earth experience was "just" a game we had once created. Through the process of reconnecting and remembering, we'd raise our consciousness and complete the game successfully.

No matter where you are at this point in time, know that you are a powerful being. By strengthening your relationship with your higher self and accessing that higher consciousness within, you can transform into the best possible version of yourself. By reconnecting within, you'll fulfill your unique life purpose and manifest your deepest dreams and desires. ("Fulfilling your soul's purpose" is another way of saying, "rising to the challenge.") And as we complete this long, long cycle of human experiencing (that culminated on the winter solstice of December 2012), a new experience for all of God's creatures will now be possible.

Rising to the challenge will take courage, of course, as your wisdom and purpose may lead you in directions that go against the established structures of society. (But notice how what's going on in the world right now is helping you muster up that courage.) However, you don't need to become a Mother Theresa or a Gandhi; you have your own contributions based on your individual gifts and talents, which you will access by strengthening the relationship with your higher self.

Human beings have both a common, general purpose (to learn, to grow emotionally and spiritually, etc.) as well as a specific purpose based on individual identity. Only you know what that is, and no one can tell you what to do. You'll discover the specifics of your individual purpose by reconnecting within and gaining trust in that inner connection. Remember that since your higher self had planned your life, including your biggest challenges, you have the knowing and the capacity within you to resolve all those challenges successfully.

When you muster up the courage to strengthen the relationship with, and integrate with, your higher self (the true Holy Spirit) by following through, you'll be of service to the whole rather than separate sectors of society. Your higher self is how you're connected to All That Is and the way to unity on an inner, as well as an outer, level. And unity and wholeness within will lead to unity and wholeness in the outer world.

The world is the way it is and circumstances are the way they are so that we can discover who we really are. We have the capacity to fulfill our deepest dreams by following our inner guidance. We can't fail if we follow this guidance. This inner power, the soul's power, is what will turn this planet around, and nothing else. The timing is perfect for this transformation to occur.

To summarize this chapter, the following are the top three reasons why you can be optimistic about your future:

1. **Your higher self, your soul, is ultimately in charge of what's going on in your life**

And to transform your life, which your higher self wants to do, strengthen your relationship with it.

2. **Your higher self is on track with Divine Plan**

Regardless of what your life may look like in the moment, it is going according to your higher self's plan (which itself fits perfectly into the larger divine plan).

3. **The Divine Plan is on track for the "New Earth"**

Within the divine design are elements that assure a "New Earth," a "Golden Age" for humanity. (There are many names for this time that's coming; Father Moore would call it, freedom, equality and brother/sisterhood.) The more you can access your higher self, the more you'll understand what's going on in your life and in the world, the less afraid you'll be, the more empowered you'll be, and the quicker you'll experience your own "Golden Age."

Your soul will always learn and grow. That is a given. However, isn't it heartening that we are transitioning from learning through pain to learning through joy? And no matter how far along in the spiritual transformation process you may be, you'll grow by leaps and bounds by strengthening your relationship with your higher self—your direct access to God, the Universe.

I'm completing this chapter with an excerpt from a message for humanity from SaLuSa of the Galactic Federation, channeled on 09-09-09 by medium Mike Quinsey. Even though I'm updating this book December of 2016 I decided to keep it here, as the message is timeless, and summarizes and complements this chapter well.

Furthermore, I appreciate that this message does not predict specific events, as some channeled messages do. Because really, no one knows exactly how specific events will play out and no one knows when, not even beings in other dimensions. The best way to predict the future is to help create it, by using fully the resources available to you when you strengthen your relationship with your higher self and fulfill your higher purpose.

"You have come a long way in a relatively short time, and the result of your dedication and determination will bring the result you seek. Ascension is for those of you who have stepped upon the lighted path that lifts you out of the lower vibrations. The reality you envisage will be more than you can imagine, and your consciousness levels will increase rapidly. Already many of you are able to think and act from your heart center, and your Light shines out as proof of your upliftment. This gladdens our hearts and tells us most certainly

that Man has created a pathway out of duality. You have become the Way-showers, and have set the pattern for others to follow . . .

"All that you need will come to you, if you continue your aspirations to spiritually evolve. For those who seek help there is no lack of assistance that will guide you onwards. Many, many souls have especially incarnated, to make the closing of this cycle as successful as can possibly be. The White Brotherhood has sent many Masters to spread the truth, and present you with the facts concerning Ascension. Dear Ones, seek and ye shall find that which resonates with you . . .

"God has not left you to flounder helplessly in the darkness that has beset Earth. Indeed, there is never a time that God is not with you and hears your prayers, and responds in ways that will help you. God is not to be feared, and on the contrary, should be thanked for the assurance that you will not be destroyed in some cataclysm. It has been decreed how this cycle shall end, and only God can decide otherwise. You can therefore go forward with absolute trust and belief in the process of Ascension that shall end your time in duality. No threats or occurrences can alter that which has been divinely decreed . . .

"We will tell you again; that every effort you put in to ascend will be more than rewarded. Your gains will be vastly more than your expectations. Heaven is a word that describes what awaits you, but it is a reality that is alive with

opportunity and exciting adventures. You certainly will not spend your time resting on clouds, as the higher dimensions are energetic and full of action. As an ascended Being you have the Cosmos as your playground, and it stretches into Infinity . . .

"You are receiving many messages from more sources than ever, and providing you exercise your wisdom and carefully consider all facts, you will avoid being misled. Stick to your preferred understanding until you find a greater truth to replace it with.

"I am SaLuSa from Sirius, and on behalf of the Galactic Federation I am always pleased to present my views to you. They are measured for your enlightenment, as we do realize that they cannot meet each of you at your own level of understanding. However, we believe there is always something to be gained from contact with you in this way. We speak to you with love in our hearts, and our energy travels with the very words we use."

Thank you SaLuSa, from Mike Quinsey

What Will Happen in the Next Several Years

You may be wondering what we can expect to have happen in the several years. Certainly, there will be changes in the way we perceive our experiences on this planet as well as changes that will manifest on many levels in many areas. However, how fast you see the changes in your own life is up to your higher life plan and how much effort you put into fulfilling it. It has taken me over 15 years from the time I first became aware of the necessity of discovering my higher purpose to get to where I am today, the beginning of 2017.

Your divine purpose is to become a spiritual master, to transcend the collective mind control (the collective illusion we've created) so that you carve your own path and come through with your unique contribution toward the New Earth. No one can tell you exactly what to do or how to do it; no one knows your unique plan. You will know what to do (and when to do it) when you connect with your higher self and follow through with your inner guidance.

However, I'd like to add an important caveat here: You may wish to receive some guidance from a good spiritual intuitive from time to time as this can be very helpful, especially when you feel stuck or when things seem like they're not moving fast enough for you. (I do this myself two or three times a year.)

In fact, the Google Adwords guru and author of *Evolution 2.0* (about the Intelligent Design of the Universe) Perry Marshall advises his clients to get a "Word from God," or a "Memo from the Head Office," as he calls them. And he says that sometimes, this Word may happen to come through a friend, or a spiritual intuitive.

In one of his emails to his community, Perry writes:

"Force yourself to add time to your day to 'listen.'

"Listen to what, you may ask?

"Whatever you may call it. I call it God. I listen for words from God every day. And I seek out words from my friends who also 'listen.' In fact, listening to these words has had a more profound impact on my life and business than just about anything else."—Perry Marshall.

I have a friend named Jahde who calls me with a "Word" for me from time to time. She's the one who told me back in the summer of 2009, when she and her daughter picked me up and took me to her house in the Santa Cruz mountains for the weekend, that I must write a second book. On the drive over I resisted the idea (No fucking way was I going to write a second book!) but the next morning I woke up with a plan for this book, including the idea that I could complete it in just over three months. By the way, Santa Cruz means "holy cross" in Spanish.

And once in a while, people just tell me things that happen to answer my questions, without consciously being aware that they have a "Word" for me.

When you receive guidance from spiritual intuitives or friends though, just make sure it resonates with you. Take the guidance in, let it "sit" with you a while, maybe sleep on it for a night or two, ask your higher self questions about it, and then go with what resonates with your heart.

As Father Charlie Moore would say, The answer to any question you may have will be whispered in your heart.

It is my mission and intent that you will be able to navigate your divine path and fulfill your mission and purpose much more quickly than I, with less confusion and fewer obstacles and painful struggles. However, I won't sugarcoat the situation and say that the next several years will be easy. They will not be that easy. But even though the next few years may be challenging, they'll be some of the most satisfying to ever experience—particularly if you follow your divine path.

As far as the bigger picture is concerned, I'm aware that some people have been wondering whether the Galactic Federation will come to our rescue, or assistance. Although I do not doubt that intelligent life exists in other parts of this galaxy and the universe (and there have been numerous reports of encounters), being saved by advanced off-planet beings is not the point of this Earth experiment and it is not part of divine plan. Divine beings don't need to be saved;

they can save themselves by discovering the divine power that's within.

Besides, off-planet beings will not rob you of the amazing experience of picking yourself up and saving yourself. It's my understanding that the most advanced levels of *spiritual evolution* are occurring right here, right now, on this planet. What happens here will affect the entire universe. This is why, according to many channeled sources, the whole universe seems to be interested in what's going on here.

Some teachers and channels speak of open visitation and give dates for this occurring. I understand they may visit us openly sometime; at some point there may be a "reunion" of some sort. But this will happen because they want to be with us and we're prepared for it, not because we are hopeless and helpless and need to be saved. (After all, we are they and they are us, in a sense.)

I don't know when this reunion will occur, or how. However, I am sure that by awakening to the bigger picture of humanity's journey and paying attention to the inner and outer signs, we'll receive everything we need when we need it, including whatever we need to know about beings on other planets.

The times ahead will require much of you—your insight, intuition, a high level of reasoning, courage, focus and inspired action. You'll be required to carefully discern what's put out by the media and other purveyors of information (and misinformation). You'll be subjected to intense social pressure, and will need to make some difficult choices. It'll be easier to make those kinds of choices when you have a strong connection with your higher self.

Yours is a journey of personal mastery, of mastery over your reality and of creating your reality. Remember that if you follow your true path you will succeed—after all, you are the one who wrote the story of your life. The time for true mastery has arrived, and a new world awaits you in the near future.

I'm ending this chapter with a message from SaLuSa of the Galactic Federation, channeled on July 27, 2009 by Mike Quinsey.

"The upliftment from where you are now to Christ consciousness will not be very long, as you would measure time. There are key points all along the way to that exalted state of being, and one is 2012 when there shall be a great input of energy into your solar system that will affect every living form. There will be a quantum leap in consciousness, and you shall take your place again amongst the Masters. All of this is quite natural when a solar cycle is completed, and it is as much a clearing out as a cleansing. Your dreams of moving into a higher state of being will be more than fulfilled, and will have been worth all of the occasions that you have experienced the dark side. Even that has had its benefits, and has shown you how a civilization can easily fall into the darkness without the realization of what has taken place. The fact that you have been grossly misled and have been denied your sovereignty has spurred you on to the greater understanding of your godlike power. Nothing is impossible when you are aligned with the Light, and even

now you wield power over the dark forces that is part of their demise."

Thank You SaLuSa, Mike Quinsey

Questions and Answers

The following are questions I received from members of my community (those who are on my list and receive my blog posts). Back in the summer of 2009 I asked my community what they wanted to know about 2012, the shift in consciousness and the spiritual awakening process that's occurring at this time and these are the questions they emailed me about.

Question 1.

Is your book *What Everyone Believed: A Memoir of Intuition and Awakening* available as an eBook for immediate purchase and downloading? Also, do you and/or the Council of Light access someone's higher self to let one know the reasons for turmoil and crisis in one's life? Why one suddenly has messed up? I have been recently in that crisis phase but in spite of my best efforts and intention I could not access my higher self and am left only with blaming myself for my rash, imprudent and impetuous behaviour. For the past several years I have been struggling to know my higher purpose and divine plan but in vain. Would you be able to help me out? H.R. in the U.K.

Answer:

As of October 2016 my book is finally available in Kindle version. It goes by the title, *Reconnected: A Spiritual Awakening Memoir*. I changed the title so that hopefully a potential reader will have a better understanding of what's in the book, and for it to be found more easily.

As far as accessing someone's higher purpose, I do not give these kinds of readings and I do not receive and transmit information from higher sources for others. Furthermore, I'm not sure whether Flo Aeveia Magdalena—the woman who channeled messages from the Counsel of Light for me—gives any more personal readings from the Counsel of Light. However, she does currently channel other beings such as "The Nameless Ones"—whose name (or lack thereof) seems to suggest they did not physically experience lifetimes on this planet.

I was honored to receive a dozen readings with the Counsel of Light over the course of several years, but this is because we were collaborating on an important project (this book being part of that project). Years ago, they said that they would eventually "integrate into the consciousness of the One"—which I am sure can be misinterpreted to mean all sorts of mystical things but which I feel means that they will no longer be separated from us and therefore there will be no need to channel them. Because . . . why channel your neighbor when you can simply walk across the street and meet with him or her in person?

You may want to have a conversation with a spiritual counselor about your situation to gain some insight that you perhaps may not get on your own. With a one-on-one conversation, you might discover and release the blocks that keep you stuck. Some of these blocks can simply be beliefs you have, beliefs that you might not be aware of as beliefs because you view them as reality, or as new age wisdom. For example: A million people meditating or thinking about peace at the same time will somehow manifest peace on the planet. (Well, you know by now that meditation is just the beginning of the process of creating peace.)

There are many good spiritual counselors, intuitives, and channels. If you want a personal reading, I'd recommend a "soul reading" with Toni Elizabeth Sar'h Petrinovich in Washington State. The reading (about 45 minutes to one hour) will give you clues to your soul's origins and purpose. However, to fulfill your higher purpose you must reconnect to your guidance directly and follow through. (Besides Toni and Flo Aeveia, I don't have any experience with others who do "soul readings.") And if you're looking for a spiritual counselor or intuitive, I'd wholeheartedly recommend Pamela Leach in Michigan. (Look for Toni and Pamela online.) Also, ask around for a good intuitive in your city or town, or visit a new age or spiritual store near you.

This book explains what you need to know and empowers you to move forward quickly in your spiritual awakening process. My first book *What Everyone Believed* (or the Kindle version, *Reconnected: A Spiritual Awakening Memoir*) will help with many additional practical examples, for understanding how I came to make sense of my life, and how you can make sense of yours, too.

In the meantime, know that your crises are helping you grow spiritually and to discover your inner gifts, inner resources—because, here you are re-examining things, being more introspective and thoughtful, and asking for guidance. By doing these things, you are headed in the right direction. Although you may not feel that you're on the right path when you're in the midst of the turmoil, once you begin the practice of reconnecting and following your inner guidance, the changes (inner and outer) that at first seem so subtle will over time become huge. I have faith that you will eventually be grateful for your difficult experiences. However, how fast this happens is up to you, and your higher self.

Question 2.

The 2012 phenomenon is the perfect event for everyone to overlay their deepest desires, fears, biases, etc. I have read a lot about it but your perspective I know will be uniquely you and to the point. I have heard so many wild overlays, but I believe it will be a rather mild non-event.

Do you think during and after that time the "veil" between us and the spirit world will be even "thinner" in the sense that for those who want to (and perhaps many that don't) it will be easier and quicker to be unequivocally in touch with their soul? This has been my desire and practice for some time. And like you, I believe that a full communication with one's soul is the answer to every question and the portal for every desire. However, even with all my knowledge and experience, I have yet to achieve that full connection. Anonymous

Answer:

You are correct in saying that the time of the "great shift in consciousness" is the perfect event for stirring up everyone's deepest desires (and fears). Humanity's greatest desire is that this time (unlike previous cycles of human experiencing and the rise and fall of civilizations) will manifest our deepest desires of peace, Oneness, and happiness.

However, there are many reasons, currently visible all around us, for people to be afraid right now—many systems in society, including the political and economic systems, appear to be breaking down. More and more people today seem to be experiencing a sense of doom or hopelessness because the world around them has become confusing and disorienting. With increasing tensions from global tragedies, over a decade of war, and divisive elections poll after poll shows that people are losing faith in many things, from government to religion. And everything from government to religion is highly polarized.

The world is ready for transformation. This book helps with that transformation by providing a higher-level perspective from which to understand the human journey, as well as the tools to transform your individual life by helping you develop a strong relationship with your higher self—your "portal" to the divine. This is what's needed to transform your life, and then the world will follow.

Not only will the "veil" between the spirit world and the physical world be thinner, you will become integrated with your higher self so that it no longer feels like something mysterious or foreign to you but simply as "you." (This "Oneness within" is one important way of viewing the concept of Oneness.)

A full connection takes time. It took me years of struggle, of experimenting, observing and figuring things out. (And it wasn't until I got strong confirmation of my connection from the Universe in the form of favorable synchronicities and new insights that answered my questions that I was satisfied that I had "made it.") It is my hope that the resources I provide will guide you to attain that deep connection much more quickly and easily than I.

My thoughts on the "veil": The veil is an illusion. There is no physical "veil." The veil is the illusion, and the illusion is the veil. The veil is imaginary, and has been imagined, "made up." We made it up. The only veil that exists, exists in one's mind and in the collective consciousness.

Question 3.

What is your interpretation of the event or events that will unfold on December 21, 2012, and how or what should we be doing to prepare for it? Thank you and have a wonderful day, J. S.

Answer:

There was a huge misunderstanding in the spiritual community that the transformation of humanity's consciousness would occur in one day, due to some "event" on December 21, 2012 that would affect humanity. I'm sure you're aware of the truth now, after reading this book.

To answer your question, the best way to prepare for the end of this cycle and the beginning of the next is by following the instructions in chapter three of this book. The instructions will help you reconnect to that part of you that's been around forever, and this will help you with what to do.

Once you gain confidence in the connection with your higher self (your direct access to the universe, to God, to the "Holy Spirit," to Interconnectedness), you'll know what to do, when to do it, what to eat and what not to eat, whether—or not—to get that flu shot, and so on. You are a sovereign being and you'll know what to do when you look within. (And yes, do your research, too. Do your research and then look into your heart ...)

Over the years, I've seen that some of the information I needed to be able to move forward in my work came to me on a "just-in-time, as needed" basis. This will continue to happen as we transform our world.

Question 4.

What is the significance of 2012? Please advise. Cheers, W.

Answer:

I hope with this book that I have answered your question to your satisfaction. Although I tried to explain as clearly as possible, please understand that you'll gain more clarity and understanding after you experience certain events firsthand and integrate them into your life. (One of the "events" I am referring to is a clear understanding of your unique contribution to the beginning of the next phase in humanity's experiencing.)

Question 5.

What will happen to those who resist the changes and continue to hold onto the old ways? Kind regards, S.

Answer:

It's best not to focus too much on what others are or aren't doing. Rather than focusing on others, begin the path of your higher purpose and then you'll be able to help others by leading by example.

Of course, your higher purpose involves you stepping into your power and speaking your truth and taking action whenever necessary (for example, when someone's behavior is dangerous to themselves or others, or inappropriate). By gaining trust in your inner guidance, you'll develop a good sense of knowing when to speak up, when to take appropriate action and when to hold back. Furthermore, once you've gotten past the "critical mass" stage of your process, you'll begin to see the perfection in the divine design, and then you will no longer be overly concerned with what others may or may not be doing. It does not mean your concern will completely vanish, but another's actions will trigger less of an emotional response from you. (And you'll be able to deal with the situation more effectively.)

And . . . is there more you could be bringing, more you could be sharing with others? Complaining about others often drove me to search for a deeper solution or to step up my efforts in my own higher purpose. You have been called to help transform the world in your own unique way, through your unique perspective. I honor your commitment and your dedication to help others and challenge you to follow your path to the best of your ability.

When others can no longer reconcile their beliefs with reality, they will find that it no longer makes sense for them to hold onto their old ways. This is the plan. Until then, it's best to reserve any judgments about others' roles. You do not know what role someone has in the divine plan. Most definitely, it's not the same as yours. I have trust in the divine design and know that things will turn out for the whole in the end.

Question 6.

I have a few questions about preparation for the "Great Shift." Will you be laying some foundational information about the "shift" itself? Perhaps more detail than your August 2008 article "The Truth About Awakening—Reconnecting with the Higher Self." If so, would you consider going into greater detail about how the planets and the Aquarian age are effectively pouring into us the energies for heightening our self-discovery and enlightenment? It's hard to find a source that is both detailed and clear at the same time.

Will your manual include health information, such as diet, supplements, and herbs that cleanse and strengthen our body's ability for absorbing and assimilating Higher Current? The greater our ability to handle this, the higher our evolving. Thanks again. W.

Answer:

I hope this book has answered your questions. I feel that the planetary and cosmic alignments are metaphors for what's happening on the Earth and in the universe at this time. I am assuming that the "energies" you are referring to here are the energies of higher consciousness. (The term "energy" may be a code word used by sources to mean higher consciousness, or higher self. Higher consciousness can also mean knowledge or wisdom. "Vibration" may be a code word for attitude, for "where you're coming from," or for sound or spoken words.) In that case, these forms of "energies" will naturally expand our self-discovery and enlightenment, and as this happens the life force energy within us will also increase.

The "Great Shift" begins with the shift that happens when you reconnect to the source of your higher consciousness—your higher self. As you reconnect and follow through and learn to trust in that connection, your attitude, behavior, and understanding all begin to shift. Your transformation then contributes to the "Great Shift" in the world.

Part of this shift will include a change in the way you eat, of course. When you become more conscious about the food you eat, you'll tend to avoid the stuff that harms your body. As you reconnect to your higher self, you'll naturally gravitate toward healthier habits because that's what you'll prefer. You will, for example, lose weight more naturally and easily, as the issues (emotional, spiritual, stress-related) that have kept the weight on will be reduced and released.

Nutrition is not my area of expertise but I'm knowledgeable enough to recommend Drs. Joseph Mercola MD, Mark Hyman, MD, Ronald Hoffman MD, Peter Glidden ND, Joel Wallach DVM, ND and JJ Virgin. They're experts in the area of nutrition and health. (Naturopathic physicians actually *study* nutrition in medical school.)

And if you want to learn about the raw food diet I recommend David Wolfe and Roger Haeske. (Dr. Mercola recommends that 50% of your diet consists of raw, uncooked fresh fruits and vegetables.)

I'm assuming by "Higher Current" you mean higher consciousness, greater life force, the creative energy flowing within you, and greater awareness. I believe it's all related.

Question 7.

My rational mind appears to be in opposition to what my heart and soul recognize as the coming truth. I would like to know how to prepare my mind to reconcile with the changes that are on their way. It's the mental push back that generates fear for me, which is in opposition to how I truly feel and not how I want to experience life. I do not wish to operate from fear. How do I let go of fear in my mind in order to fully embrace the wholeness of love? Thanks, M.

Answer:

The best way to "prepare the human mind" is to follow the guidelines for reconnecting with your higher consciousness in this book and to try to better understand the human journey, the bigger picture. The combination of the two, the trust in yourself and in the divine plan (that will develop within you as you follow this path) will help reduce your fear.

Question 8.

Angelic Oracle Kira Ra and Wisdom Teacher Sri Ram Ka put on a convention for 2012. I also attended the Oneness University in India, where they speak of the transformation of human consciousness. They are also oriented towards 2012. The show they put on doesn't always correspond with reality, though.

I have no idea what's going on and what 2012 will bring. Mankind is in deep confusion, and lost in layers of mud. Being that the mud is the transitory stuff of the human mind, perhaps we will rise from the mud in an instant, or not! Personally, I am struggling to put my life back together after divorce and to earn enough money to survive. I do pray for my daughter's sake that mankind, and myself, will find the way to transform coal into diamonds. Have a beautiful day, F.

Answer:

You have a beautiful way of putting it! I know that we will rise from the mud in what will turn out to be the blink of an eye (compared to the amount of time we spent in the mud, in fallen consciousness). The confusion is there for a good reason—so that we examine, reassess and transform our lives. So that we bring our hearts and minds into alignment, and into alignment with the new paradigm that's emerging—and create a New Earth. By following your path, you'll discover your unique gifts that will bring you outer success while contributing to the Golden Age for humanity.

I'm not familiar with the wisdom teachers you mention or with Oneness University. But I do understand that each of us in our unique way is helping bring humanity closer to having our deepest dreams and desires fulfilled.

Question 9.

1. Are recent energy manifestations such as an activation of electro-magnetic energy, a Leyline with a large vortex within the Jumping Pound Creek Valley in Cochrane, Alberta an indication of the Earth's responding to the "Great Shift?" 2. Is this also part of the activation of such sites as Lake Louise, Lake O'Hara, Peyto Lake, and Emerald Lake—a complex within Banff and Yoho National Parks? 3. How would it be best to personally participate within these natural areas to get the most beneficial "growth"? 4. Are these forces there to help us to experience the changes and for our individual transformation? If so, how can we best participate? Blessings, R.F.

Answer:

I'm not sure I can answer your questions to your satisfaction as I'm not that knowledgeable about the Earth's ley lines. However, if ley lines are to the Earth as meridians in Chinese medicine are to the human body, I can certainly get that being in an area of increased ley-line concentration can be beneficial for increasing one's energy and therefore one's growth. I've found that being in nature and touching the Earth as directly as possible has helped me relax and get in touch with my deeper wisdom, so much so that I've maintained a daily practice of hiking in a natural area for over nine years. It's easier to get in touch with your higher self and your wisdom when you are in nature (than when you're watching television in a noisy apartment complex, for example). If I were you and lived near Banff, I'd visit that area often.

Having said that, you do not need to go out of your way to specific places to get transformed—unless you are called to do so by your inner guidance. You can and will be able to transform yourself anywhere. Not everyone needs to visit Banff to be transformed. Not everyone has to attend specific workshops to be transformed. I enjoyed attending workshops but I found that when you get on the path of your divine purpose, you can't help but grow really fast.

By the way, workshops and special gatherings and ceremonial events can be fun and often helpful, but some aren't as powerful as claimed. Most of the growth and transformation happens "in the trenches," in your real life. And that's what ultimately makes the difference.

Question 10.

1. Will all people have the same effects of 2012? What is the effect? 2. Some people claim DNA connection (activation) is helpful. How? 3. Ascension seems to be associated with 2012. Is this physical, mental or what? How does it work? Clarifying 2012 is a good idea. Thanks for your help. M.

Answer:

The effect is an increase in awareness through reconnecting with higher consciousness, with your heart (as Father Charlie Moore would say). A greater awareness will have many favorable consequences, including fulfilling your higher purpose and experiencing an increase in health, peace, love, freedom, cooperation and joy. While not all people will begin to see and feel these effects at the same time, eventually no one will escape being affected by them.

Whether you choose to do a DNA activation or not is up to you. I've had a "Circuitry Alignment" done once, but I'm not sure I noticed any significant effects. I feel it may be similar to going to a workshop—there may be some positive effects by participating, but much more is available to you when you activate your own awakening. It makes sense that no one can activate your DNA for you, that you activate your own DNA by reconnecting to your higher consciousness and learning to trust in that connection. And it makes sense that your active participation in raising your own awareness is what's required here.

Ascension refers to the shift in consciousness from "lower level" human consciousness to include the consciousness of your higher self. You ascend in your consciousness without having to "lose" your physical body. You attain higher-level consciousness without having to return to the "place" between incarnations. I hope this book has helped you with shifting your consciousness.

Question 11.

My partner and I have been recently introduced to the investigative research of William Henry. I think you will find him very informative. He touches on the subject of Mayan prophecy of 2012, on the workings of our inner self, which he calls "spiritual technology," and also our past association with various civilizations.

Investigative mythologist William Henry describes Light Beings as ancient enlightened ones who came to Earth and left a spark of themselves inside us. The Light Body is the name given to our hidden spiritual body and is referenced in many sacred traditions, he explains. The Mayans prophesized that enlightened beings would emerge from a serpent rope (possibly a star-gate or wormhole) from the center of our galaxy in 2012, and Egyptian traditions also speak of beings of light, he noted.

Is humankind on the verge of discovering the primordial secrets of God—seeing the light of first creation? Ultimately, humans have the ability to transform themselves through consciousness into light beings, Henry asserts. Blessings, K.

Answer:

I am not familiar with William Henry, but anyone can find a wealth of information on the shift in consciousness on the Internet. Everyone who writes about the shift in consciousness and the transformation that we're on the brink of at this time has a slightly different angle and interpretation. Some emphasize the Mayan culture connection, while others focus on the physical and astronomical phenomena. Still others channel "ascended masters" or star beings that attempt to enlighten people with a higher-level perspective. I feel that most everyone's interpretation contains parts of the truth, but no one has the entire picture yet.

What I've attempted with this book is to synthesize the available information in order to make more sense of what it all means, and to empower people to make the shift within by providing detailed guidelines for how to strengthen the relationship with their higher self so that they become masters of their lives, and shamans. I feel this is the most important aspect of the human experience at this point in time and what we need to focus on.

When you reconnect with your higher consciousness, gain confidence in that connection and begin to see the bigger picture of humanity's evolutionary journey, you'll be much more able to discern the information that comes your way. You will not be so easily manipulated by all the hype and propaganda that's in your face because you'll be reconnected with your higher consciousness, your very own built-in (but until recently, dormant) B.S. detector. Remember that certain establishments have an interest in maintaining the status quo. (The Empire has not disappeared, just changed form.)

You'll also begin to see the metaphors in ancient prophecies. For example, did you ever think that you may have been one of the ancient enlightened ones who came to Earth eons ago? Do you know that you already have a Light Body (your higher self)? You most likely had at least one lifetime in Atlantis. And . . . the Mayans are correct in prophesizing that "2012" will bring the emergence of enlightened beings on this planet: us. (By the way, the serpent rope symbolizes the DNA helix and the spiraling up of your energy as you raise your consciousness.)

Question 12.

1. What is your prime motivation for writing this book? 2. Are you aware of how much your ego will be influencing what you write, and have means to counter that? We are not our ego. Ego is a survival tool. In my opinion, anyone with ego arrogance will not even be able to go through the shift. 3. How much does the thought of what people will think influence your words, or will you trust that spirit will guide your hand through your heart?

How you answer these questions will greatly affect your personal experience through the shift. Learning to communicate with your guides or higher self will expedite your growth and will be the greatest action you can take for yourself. Sincerely, J.

Answer:

My prime motivation for writing this book is to help others through the process of reconnecting with their higher self, their spiritual awakening. At the same time, I'm clear that my needing to support myself (and my family) has been motivating me to plug away at this project daily so that it gets done sooner rather than later. These two motivating factors assure that I will get my understandings out there in a timely manner, as my tendency is to be reserved—as many engineers are. But now it's time to speak up.

This is also why I've updated this book from a "2012-based" title (which I sold on my website from 2009 through the end of 2016) to a more relevant title with availability on Amazon Kindle ... so that more people can access it, gain comfort from it, and transform their life and their world.

We are spiritual beings experiencing physical life. We may not be our ego, but we use the ego (mind) to experience life. When you go through the shift you'll become aware of how much your ego serves and has been serving as a vehicle for your soul to learn, grow, accumulate wisdom and express itself, and then you'll have fewer issues with it. The ego will become a non-issue.

The shift happens when you shift your consciousness from the level of the personality / ego / mind to **include** the consciousness of your higher self. The shift will not negate or knock the ego because, as you stated, the ego / mind is a survival tool and you'll need your mind to function in order for your body to survive. (Remember that this time we are ascending with bodies intact.) I cover a bit about the ego and the nonsense that's been written about it in my first book *What Everyone Believed: A Memoir of Intuition and Awakening* (hardcover version) and *Reconnected: A Spiritual Awakening Memoir* (Kindle version). In that book I also share my confusion around my own issues of arrogance and how I dealt with ego as well.

Rather than knocking the ego, it's much better to focus our energy on reconnecting to our higher self and dealing with the issues of fear and false beliefs (ego / mind issues) that will inevitably come up. You are correct in stating that developing a relationship with your higher self will be the best thing you can do for yourself.

I understand that if I don't ruffle people's feathers, I'm not contributing to humanity's growth. I also understand that although we are all equal, we are all in different stages of growth and it's okay that others happen to disagree. (This is also by divine plan.) I will not dilute what I share for fear of what others will think, although I'm aware that how I present this information and the order in which it is presented is very important.

Thank you for reading my book.

Thank You!

I hope you've enjoyed this book and are armed with some tools and insights to help you strengthen your relationship with your higher self and raise your spiritual awareness.

I'd appreciate it very much if you could review this book on Amazon. Has this book helped you? Have you experienced any interesting synchronicities or new insights after reading it? How has it made a difference in your life? Your feedback will help others decide if this book is right for them.

And if you'd like to learn more about the reconnecting and awakening process my first book, *What Everyone Believed: A Memoir of Intuition and Awakening* (Kindle title: *Reconnected: A Spiritual Awakening Memoir*) will give you a nitty-gritty, nuts and bolts account of one person's journey through the process, including insights that will help you on your journey and reduce your fear of change.

Many thanks and have a wonderful spiritual journey!

Christine

About the Author

It's not only important but critical that each of us bring our soul's wisdom to this world full of chaos, distrust and unease. This is why Christine Hoeflich has chosen to follow her inner and outer nudges ... so she could make a difference in the world—as well as for her family—in these most interesting of times.

Christine is the author of *What Everyone Believed: A Memoir of Intuition and Awakening* (the original hardcover title; *Re-connected: A Spiritual Awakening Memoir* is the Kindle title) and *Activating 2012: A Practical Guide for*

Navigating 2012 with Confidence and Clarity (updated version titled, *The Spiritual Awakening Process: Coming Out of the Darkness and Into the Light*.) A former materials engineer, she has developed the steps needed for strengthening the relationship with our higher self, gaining trust in our intuition, accessing Interconnectedness, and understanding our soul's bigger plan.

Her memoir, *What Everyone Believed: A Memoir of Intuition and Awakening,* was recognized by Publisher North Atlantic Books as "One of 4 Notable Spiritual Awakening Memoirs," along with *Eat Pray Love*, *The Happiness Project,* and *Star Sister*.

Christine has written articles, blogged and tweeted on spiritual awakening and personal growth. About nine months after setting up her Twitter account, she was recognized by Mashable in their article, "Nonfiction Tweets: 70+ Authors to Follow on Twitter," in the Creative Nonfiction category.

She was also recognized by CreativeClass.com (online college degrees) in their article, "100 Amazingly Insightful People You Can Learn from on Twitter," in the Words of Wisdom and Inspiration" category, next to Oprah and Deepak Chopra.

Christine has a blog where she writes about spiritual awakening at ChristineHoeflich.com. You may reach her through her blog.

Please take a moment to review this book on Amazon. She'll be very grateful.

Printed in Germany
by Amazon Distribution
GmbH, Leipzig